SEED TO WEED

STONE

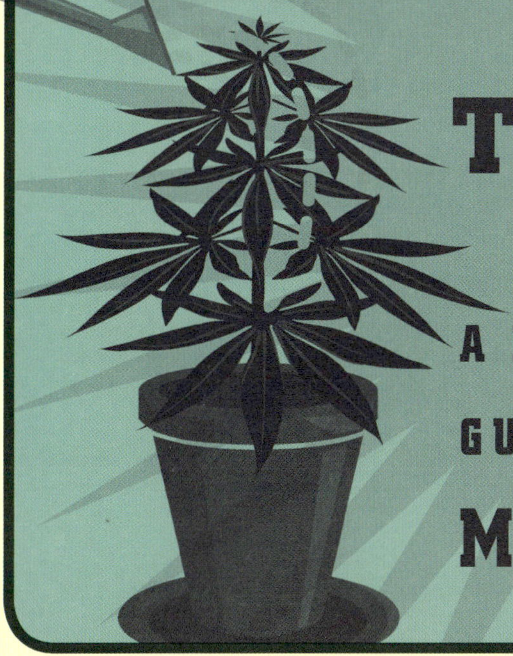

A POT ENTHUSIAST'S GUIDE TO GROWING MARIJUANA

TEN SPEED PRESS
Berkeley

Copyright © 2012 by
Elephant Book Company Limited

Illustrations copyright © 2012 by
Elephant Book Company Limited

All rights reserved.

Published in the United States by Ten Speed Press, an imprint of the Crown Publishing Group, a division of Random House, Inc., New York, by arrangement with Elephant Book Company Limited, 35 Fournier Street, London E1 6QE, United Kingdom

www.crownpublishing.com
www.tenspeed.com

Ten Speed Press and the Ten Speed colophon are registered trademarks of Random House, Inc.

Editorial Director: Will Steeds
Project Editor: Laura Ward
Cover and Interior Design: Lindsey Johns
Illustrator: Robert Brandt
Copy Editor: Elisabeth Beller
Production: Robert Paulley
Color Reproduction:
Modern Age Repro House Ltd., Hong Kong

Ten Speed Press Editor: Lisa Regul

Library of Congress Cataloging-in-Publication Data

Stone, Chris, 1973–

From seed to weed : a pot enthusiast's guide to growing marijuana / Chris Stone. — 1st ed.

   p. cm.

1. Cannabis. 2. Marijuana. 1. Title.

SB295.C35S745 2012

633.7'9—dc23

                       2011026602

ISBN 978-1-60774-109-1

Printed in China

10 9 8 7 6 5 4 3 2 1

First Edition

SEED TO WEED

Contents

Introduction 6

Chapter 1: Say High to Mary Jane 8

Chapter 2: Preparing to Grow 20

Chapter 3: Grow-Room Kit and Setups 34

Chapter 4: Let's Get Growing 60

Chapter 5: Harvesting and Curing 92

Chapter 6: Starting Over 108

Chapter 7: Troubleshooting 120

Acknowledgments 128

Introduction

Hey, there. Welcome to the Wonderful World of Growing Your Own Weed. If you've bought this book I guess it's fair to assume that you are partial to more than the occasional cannabis cigarette. But in growing terms, you're probably a virgin. The good news is that growing cannabis at a basic level is not a complicated process. After all, it grows naturally all over America and other parts of the world—it's called "weed" for a reason.

There's a hell of a lot of information out there—in books and on the Web—about growing. There are some epic publications (naming no names) that cover in almost infinite detail everything you and generations of your descendants would ever want to know about marijuana horticulture. My intention with this book is to keep things nice 'n' easy.

WHY GROW YOUR OWN WEED?

There are three main reasons. The first is convenience. If you are buying your pot from a dealer, you are beholden to him or her. If your stash is running low and you can't get hold of him, during one of his stays at the local penitentiary, you need to find another source or go cold turkey. The second is quality. You may be one of the few who knows his dealer well, but if your contact is just a link in a chain, how do you know the conditions in which your purchase has been grown? The third is cost. Like anything in life, if you have to buy goods or a service because you are unable to do or make something yourself, you will invariably pay more.

"If you substitute marijuana for tobacco and alcohol, you'll add eight to twenty-four years to your life."

—**Jack Herer, Writer and Pro-hemp Campaigner**

Your brains are probably addled anyway from all that bong action, and given that you never managed to trawl through much reading in high school, why would you start now?

Many cannabis experts would have you believe that you need a multitude of expensive equipment to start a weed garden, from halide lights and dehumidifiers to complex irrigation systems, but this should only really be the preserve of the large-scale commercial grower. This book is aimed at the novice grower who wants to grow anywhere between one and five plants—enough to keep you and a few buddies nicely baked until the next harvest. Or, if you're a medical marijuana patient, enough to make cakes or savories to share 'round your collective. Hell, you can even grow a single plant on a window ledge if you want. Think slim budget, small scale, and low key . . . which will save you money, save you hassle, and keep you under the cops' radar.

I welcome you to the cannabis-growing fraternity. In these pages you'll find out about growing from seeds and clones, the all-important growth stages, how to set up basic indoor and outdoor gardens, harvesting, troubleshooting, and much more. And we'll start with some basic orientation about the plant itself.

May you have fun developing your green fingers.

Chris Stone

DISCLAIMER

It is a criminal offense in parts of the United States and in many other countries, punishable by imprisonment and/or fines to cultivate, possess, or supply cannabis. You should therefore understand that this book is intended for private amusement and not intended to encourage you to break the law.

INTRODUCTION

chapter 1
SAY HIGH TO MARY JANE

"Why is marijuana against the law? It grows naturally upon our planet. Doesn't the idea of making nature against the law seem to you a bit . . . unnatural?"

—Bill Hicks, comedian

There is a lot that can be (and indeed has been) written about the genetic makeup of the cannabis plant. I'm certainly not going to repeat too much of it here, but there are certain facts you need to know. The better you understand the plant, the better the chronic you will cultivate. Time to get serious and make some notes.

Cannabis: A Potted History

Mankind has been using cannabis for thousands of years. And that's a fact. In 2005, a clay beaker featuring cannabis twine as part of its design was discovered in China. Archeologists dated it at approximately ten thousand years old.

The cannabis plant is thought to have originated in the Himalayas. From there it spread throughout Asia and into the Middle East and Africa, and today it grows wild all over the world.

Successive civilizations embraced this versatile plant. It was used to make medicines, parchment, clothing, ropes, tents, and eaten as food by humans and livestock. And it wasn't long before the holy men of various religions also noted its mind-altering powers as a drug. As the ancient Chinese book, the *Pên Ching*, noted: "If one takes it over a long period of time one can communicate with the spirits and one's own body becomes light." Those Chinese dudes knew how to party.

Indeed the birth of the modern United States is thought to be based, in no small part, on the not-so-humble cannabis plant—in 1620 the founding fathers reportedly set sail on the *Mayflower* with bags of hemp seed on board. And it was clearly popular. In 1794, America's first president, George Washington, famously remarked: "Make the most of hemp seed. Sow it everywhere." And if it was good enough for him. . . .

HEMP USES
(CLOCKWISE FROM TOP)

- Paper
- Textiles
- Plastics
- Body care
- Construction
- Livestock food
- Livestock bedding
- Essential oils
- Nutritional supplements
- Medicines
- Food

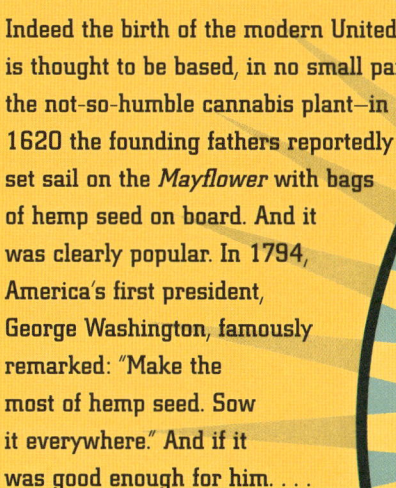

SAY HIGH TO MARY JANE

How Does Your Garden Grow?

Left to its own devices, cannabis is an annual plant (that is, it flowers and dies in a single growing season). It is the only annual plant, in fact, that is *dioecious* (meaning it has separate male and female plants). There are six main stages to its life cycle:

1 Germination. Each spring the plant germinates when the root pokes through the seed's casing. This process can take anywhere between twelve hours and three weeks.

2 Seedling. From there the plant enters the seedling stage when the stem begins to mature and several leaves appear.

3 Vegetative growth. The plant enters a period of rapid growth through the summer, when it receives the most light. The stem thickens, leaves multiply, and branches develop.

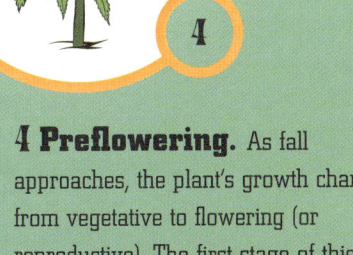

6 Seed generation. Once fertilized, the small ovary found behind each flower of the female plant begins to swell and within a few weeks, mature seeds are produced. When most of the flowers are fertilized, the plant stops producing new flowers. Its energy goes to maturing the seeds instead, and once this is done, the plant withers and dies.

5 Flowering. The reduction in available light in each twenty-four-hour period triggers flowering. The male plants produce small, white spheres that look like miniature grapes. The females produce pistils that look like tentacles. To produce seeds (from which grow the next generation), small pollen sacks on the male plants must fertilize the pistils of the female flowers. Male plants die soon after releasing pollen into the air, their life's purpose accomplished.

4 Preflowering. As fall approaches, the plant's growth changes from vegetative to flowering (or reproductive). The first stage of this is preflowering, when the plant stops growing up and starts to fill out with thicker branches and denser leaves. These large fan leaves are the lungs of the plant. At this stage the plant starts to show its sex (avert your eyes, kids).

LEGAL WEED
This type of weed is harvested all over the world for use as industrial fiber, oil, and food. It can take anywhere from ten to thirty-six weeks for a marijuana plant to complete its life cycle (from seed to full maturity). But as you will discover, this generic life cycle is a world away from the type of weed the average pothead is interested in.

Cannabis Strains

There are three different species of cannabis:

Cannabis sativa is probably the more well known of the three. It's been used for hundreds of years as an industrial fiber, seed oil, food, spiritual tool, medicine, and, of course, drug! The plant grows fairly tall (4–15 ft. [1.2–4.5 m]) and willowy. The high it delivers is, in its purest form, an intense, euphoric, cerebral high. Purple Haze and Thai are common sativa strains.

Cannabis indica is typically shorter (grows up to 4 ft. [1.2m]) and more densely branched than its sativa cousin. Thought to have originated in Pakistan and Afghanistan, it is traditionally cultivated for the production of hashish. Its genetic makeup (producing higher levels of *cannabinoids* (see "Delta Force" page 19) than sativa) results in a deeply stoned, mongy, couch-locked state. Afghani and Northern Lights are common indicas.

Sativa

Indica

Ruderalis

Crossbreeding

The description here is very black and white. In reality, few pure indica or sativa strains reach the average Joe. Such are the wonders of nature that any of these species (even ruderalis) can be crossbred with another at varying percentages to alter the genetics, complexity, and high of your smoke. For instance, Bubblegum, Super Skunk, and White Widow are all examples of sativa/indica hybrids. It's, like, messing with Nature, man. But it's for your own good.

Sativa   Indica   Ruderalis

Cannabis ruderalis flourishes in much harsher climates than either sativa or indica and does not grow as tall. Its flower cycle is based on age and not the *photoperiod* (amount of light and dark to which it is subjected), which means the grower cannot control its cycle or therefore the buds it produces. Furthermore, its weak THC content (see "Delta Force" page 19) makes it great for hemp but of little use in your bong bowl.

Getting lost among the sweet smelling leaves of this crop might be your idea of heaven, but you ain't gonna get high from it!

SAY HIGH TO MARY JANE

It's All About Sex

Relax, I'm not about to revisit that uncomfortable "chat" you had with your dad in sixth grade. Nor, alas, am I about to embark on a seedy tale of porn. This is a matter of gender. In cannabis cultivation there are effectively four genders: the standard male and female, the (woo-hoo) hermaphrodite, and sinsemilla (the *raison d'être* of the marijuana grower).

Male

In cannabis horticulture, as in life, all males are useless. Male plants contain very low levels of THC, and, while it's possible to derive a mild high from smoking male plants, they don't taste very good. But it gets worse. Rather than just doing the horticultural equivalent of sitting around drinking beer and watching college football, if left *in situ*, males will pollinate the females and slowly but surely destroy your crop. They must be stopped. The only reason (save stoned ignorance) that growers cultivate males is for pollen to make seeds.

Male flowers — If left alone, male flowers will mature (open their seed sacks) and pollinate.

Male

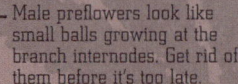

Male preflowers look like small balls growing at the branch internodes. Get rid of them before it's too late.

Males feature a raised stem.

Female

Once pollinated, the female produces THC but also seeds. These seeds inhibit its ability to grow quantities of bud. These pollinated females are also largely useless as a means of getting high.

Female

Female flowers

A female plant in full bloom. A joyous sight!

Female preflowers are easy to spot by virtue of the fuzzy white pistils which protrude from the top.

Female preflowers don't have a stem.

Hermaphrodite

Containing both male and female organs, a hermaphrodite is often created under poor growing conditions. The plant is sometimes able to pollinate itself, thereby taking on the characteristics of a female, but, like those suspicious-looking sex workers you encountered during that vacation in Thailand, these plants are best avoided.

Hermaphrodite

SAY HIGH TO MARY JANE

17

Sinsemilla (from the Spanish (*sin* [without] and *semilla* [seed]). This is the term for a *nonpollinated* female. The Holy Grail of the weed farmer, sinsemilla will produce vastly more buds with greater levels of THC than the male, seeded female, or hermaphrodite plant as it strives to attract pollen.

Playing God

So, as is now clear, to grow and harvest good quality bud, cannabis cannot simply be grown without intervention. The cannabis cultivator must "play God" and alter nature's course, depriving the female cannabis plant of the pollen she craves. In a way it's sad, but the results are oh so worth it.

Delta Force

Of course the main characteristic of the plant that you're interested in is the bit that makes you really spaced! Cannabis plants produce a psychoactive ingredient called *cannabinoids*. There are over four hundred types of cannabinoids (see box below) in marijuana plants (an alphabet soup of abbreviations from CBD and CBN to THCV). You just need to be aware of the key player in all this—the Big Cheese: *Delta-9-Tetrahydrocannabinol* (THC to you and me). This is the active ingredient in cannabis and the reason why your parents have long since given up on you getting a proper job, why the tunes you play during a session "really mean something, man," and why you have the short-term memory capabilities of the average retiree.

That's it: lecture over on the properties of cannabis. I hope you're not too giddy with this assault of information. But just in case, you'd best roll a fat one and take some time out before reading chapter 2.

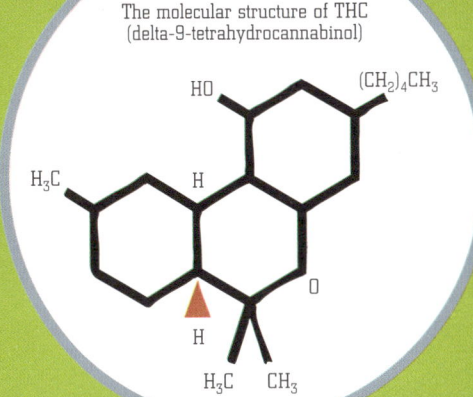

The molecular structure of THC (delta-9-tetrahydrocannabinol)

Cannabinoids

Cannabinoids are contained in the very small mushroom-like structures (*trichomes*) that cover the female flowers. Have a look at some sparkly bud at 30x magnification, and you will notice them. Sativas are generally high in THC and low in CBD; sativas with their high THC content are great for getting a cerebral buzz, and indicas with their high CBD content are great for monging out or couch-lock. CBN is produced when THC degrades. As THC levels fall (after you've harvested), the CBN levels will rise.

chapter 2: PREPARING TO GROW

"I think people need to be educated to the fact that marijuana is not a drug. Marijuana is an herb and a flower. God put it here. If He put it here and He wants it to grow, what gives the government the right to say that God is wrong?"

—Willie Nelson, singer

Before any grower starts to cultivate Mary Jane, he or she needs to plan the grow. It's no good just sticking some seeds in a pot, putting a light on them, and hoping for the best. You need to decide where to grow (indoor or outdoor), how to grow, and to consider issues such as space, budget, and, of course, security.

The Great Debate

The seismic debate within growing circles is whether to locate your garden indoors or outdoors. Circumstances may dictate that you have no choice, but if you do, here's the lowdown on the advantages and disadvantages of both.

Indoor growing undoubtedly produces the best yields (up to ten times greater than that produced by natural outdoor growing). Artificial light is far superior in producing large buds with higher concentrations of THC than natural sunlight. Also, you have complete control over the environment and are therefore able to maintain the optimum levels of heat, light, and humidity to facilitate growth—making your choice of cultivation kit (see chapter 3) all the more important. On the downside, the cost of electricity to run high-powered lights at least twelve hours a day, plus a fan to generate airflow, is expensive.

Outdoor growing is largely as nature intended. It is cheaper than indoor gardening and relatively odor free. But if you live in a climate where temperatures can fall below 59°F (15°C) or rise above 88°F (31°C) during March to October, your plants may not thrive.

So which side are you on? Once you've made your decision, you need to start planning the exact location. Typically indoor grows are more complex than outdoor ones if you wish to maximize yield.

Indoor Growing

There are various locations that cannabis can be grown in an indoor environment, from the very simple window grow space using natural light (effectively an outdoor grow space within the confines of your house) to the vast, commercial grow world of Sea of Green (SOG). SOG is a method whereby a sizeable area (sometimes a whole room, especially an attic or basement) is dedicated to growing many short plants packed tightly together.

Whatever your ambitions, all locations must have ventilation, access to electricity (for light and heat), and be of a minimum height and width (this will vary greatly depending on your chosen strain). Think privacy but also accessibility.

All houses are different, so think about what suits your property best. A ground floor street-facing window ledge makes for a bad grow area; the light may be great, but the whole world will see your handiwork while walking past. Similarly, confined spaces may be discreet but if they're too inaccessible, you will need to hire a contortionist to tend to your crop! A space 4 ft. high by 2 ft. wide and 1 ft. deep (120 cm × 60 cm × 30 cm) can easily be converted into a grow room capable of housing up to five plants—more than enough for your needs.

An attic is a great place to start a larger-scale growroom. It's warm, dry, and above all away from prying eyes.

PREPARING TO GROW

Outdoor Growing

Outdoor grows are *really* easy. After all, this is growing as God intended, and as long as you have the climate, there's not a whole lot that can go wrong. It's no more challenging than keeping some shrubs or roses alive, but the end result is far more rewarding.

There are various locations you can choose, from public woodland (see "Guerrilla growing") to a greenhouse, but whatever you choose, try to ensure the location is south facing (for the maximum exposure to sunlight) in well-draining soil. I would advocate a corner plot in your garden, well lit and protected from the worst of the wind. You could erect a simple cover made from corrugated plastic to protect your plant(s) in the early stages of development.

Make sure the grow area is secure. A wire-mesh fence will deter pests; make sure it is pinned to the ground to prevent predators from pushing underneath. If your grow patch can be seen, camouflage it with grass or bracken if possible. A high wooden fence is ideal, the better to keep out pests and guard against prying eyes.

You *can* grow from seeds outdoors but I would suggest growing seedlings indoors and transplanting to the outdoor location for vegetation onward. (See chapter 4 for more information on growing from seed.)

Your choice of plant strain will be determined by circumstance. You don't want a high-growing sativa like Durban Poison if it will tower above your short fence. Early flowering varieties that are resistant to mold and disease, like Holland's Hope and Early Girl, are a good choice for outdoor cultivation. Longer flowering and big producing varieties (e.g., Power Plant) can be victims of the damp conditions prevalent in early fall.

Don't flaunt it

Don't make the mistake made by Florida resident Bryan Hartman in 2010 who was prosecuted for growing seventeen marijuana plants, some as tall as 7 ft. (2 m), in his front yard, in full view of the road. Doh!

Guerrilla growing

You also have the option of planting your garden on land other than your own (guerrilla gardening). You should spend time while ambling through the forest smoking reefers to choose a good sunny spot in a very remote location, preferably near water. Opt for public land; you're breaking the law as it is so don't compound it by growing on private property; it's bad karma. Having said that, in parts of the United States, especially California, public land is becoming overrun with commercial grows, which are protected by gun-toting heavies. You should exercise caution with any guerrilla grow.

The big upside of guerrilla gardening is that unless you're caught red-handed at the site, and you take obvious precautions, no one can reasonably link you with the garden. The flip side is that all your hard work may be for naught if a fellow stoner stumbles across the plot close to harvest and steals your prize buds.

PREPARING TO GROW

How Much Do You Want To Grow?

Of course, if you have the space, time, and money to devote to it, there is no limit to the size of garden you can grow. But the bigger the grow area, the greater the cost (in terms of lights, ozone generators, ballasts, and pumps, to name a few), and although a bigger grow area will give you a larger crop, you may have to give away (or sell) your spare buds . . . and the harsher the sentence will be if you're caught.

So, as suggested in the introduction, your goal should be a very small garden. That means just a handful of plants at most. But how does the number of plants you pot equate to the weight of juicy bud you'll harvest? Yield is determined by several factors including genetics, but your lighting setup is key—a beginner could expect to get an ounce or two from a 125-watt CFL and about 10 oz. (283 g) from a 600-watt HID setup. An experienced grower would expect to double this—20 oz. (567 g) from just five plants! But don't get carried away, you have much to learn. . . .

The greater the number of plants you cultivate and the higher the wattage of your lighting setup, the more buds you'll get!

SEED TO WEED

Seeds For Weed

Now you've decided whether you're an indoor or outdoor cultivator and know your desired yield, it's time to give some thought to actually growing the stuff. There are two ways to cultivate cannabis—from seeds and from clones. Cloning is quicker—the plants are guaranteed to be female and the process generally leads to better results—but it does require a little expertise (see chapter 6 for a full analysis). Seed cultivation will result in a proportion of your saplings being male, but it is surely the best bet for first-time growers.

While it remains illegal to grow cannabis in the United States, UK, Europe, and elsewhere—with varying degree of punishment and with significant regional variations—it is perfectly legal to purchase cannabis seeds in the UK and some European countries. What the powers that be expect you to do with marijuana seeds if not to grow some jaw-dropping buds is not clear. But let's not dwell on that. Just be thankful that seeds are readily available on the Internet. In Europe you can walk right in to a grow shop and buy seeds over the counter. Sadly this liberal attitude does not exist in the United States (see "Buying seeds" page 30).

Choosing which seed to grow comes down to five main factors: potency (THC content), type of high, length of cycle, grow height, and price. Strains can vary significantly in all five. These factors make up the genetic imprint of the plant. If you plant a sativa variety like Haze, which has an eighteen- to twenty-week flowering time, there is nothing you can do in the cultivation process to speed this up. Similarly, there is no way to increase the bud growth or potency of your strain by adhering to some "magic formula." It is what it is, and you get what you pay for.

If you are in a hurry for a smoke (aren't we all), you could try an established indica, like Northern Lights, which can be put into flower after only four to eight weeks. If time is not an issue—your buddy may already have a couple of ounces in the freezer—but a strong strain that delivers a euphoric high is important, then a Malawi or Thai will do nicely.

Some indica varieties can be ready for flowering in as little as four weeks, whereas certain sativas can take six to nine months to go from seed to full maturity. So, if you're a man or woman in a hurry, indica is the way to go.

The table opposite lists a small cross section of the many seeds available, to help you decide.

Juicy buds, such as the ones on this plant—ripe and ready for harvest—are at your fingertips.

AUTOFLOWERING

Although it flies in the face of all accepted cannabis-growing theory, you can now obtain seeds for autoflowering strains. As the name suggests, these seeds will flower in a given time period, unaffected by the change in photoperiod. The downside is that because they have no vegetative growth period and go straight into flower, they can never produce a large yield. Autoflowering is certainly not for the purists, but it might make things a whole lot easier for a first-timer like you.

Seed types

Name	Strain	Potency (THC content)	Indoor/outdoor	Flowering period	Grow height	Approx. price (per seed)
Super Skunk	Hybrid	10%–15%	Indoor	56–63 days	2–3 ft	$6
Afghani	Indica	10%–15%	In & Out	56–63 days	3–4 ft	$7
Northern Lights	Indica	10%–15%	Indoor	56–63 days	3–4 ft	$12
Kali Mist	Sativa	14%–16%	Indoor	65–70 days	5–6 ft	$12
White Widow	Hybrid	20%–25%	In & Out	63 days	3-4 ft	$6
UK Cheese	Hybrid	20%–25%	In & Out	70 days	3-4 ft	$10

PREPARING TO GROW

Buying seeds

Once you've chosen your seed, it's time to acquire some but from where? By far the best means is from a buddy who has some from a strain you have already smoked. That way the seeds will be free and you'll pretty much know the type of high you're gonna get.

Failing that, you can purchase seeds from one of the many "banks" out there to be found on the Internet. Beware: many of these companies are rip-off merchants, while others, like the famous Sensi Seed bank, will not fulfill orders to the United States because it remains largely illegal here. However, marijuana has been legalized for medical use in fifteen states in the United States, including Alaska, California, Colorado, and Washington. So this is a loophole that can be exploited, although you didn't hear it from me.... Search the Web for "medical marijuana collectives." This can steer you onto a good source for seeds to buy locally, as long as you pretend you've got some ailment or other.

Most seed banks sell seeds in packets of between five and fifteen seeds. And the price can vary from $5 to $30 per seed. The more expensive tend to be award-winning strains, usually well-established hybrids. As with everything in life, you get what you pay for. But as a virgin grower, it's probably advisable that you start with something at the cheaper end of the scale.

If your goal is just a couple of plants, it is still advisable to plant up to ten seeds. Unless you have bought

SEED BANK HELP

If you need help separating the wheat from the chaff (or rather the trichomes from the fan leaves!) when it comes to seed banks you could do worse than take a look at Green Man's seed review website, www.seedbankupdate.com. This offers impartial ratings of many seed banks based on firsthand reviews, giving you a good idea of the levels of service and quality of product of a particular bank before you part with your hard-earned cash.

feminized seeds (see box below), it stands to reason that about half your crop will turn out to be male and those will need to be culled at the earliest opportunity. Of the remaining females, some will show more promising signs than others.

When your seeds arrive, check that none are crushed. Also take a look at the quality. Strong seeds with a good germination rate tend to be dark brown and hard to the touch. Soft, pale seeds often produce sickly plants. Contact the seller if you feel there are issues with your seeds. If all is okay, transfer the seeds from the package to a *very* dry crush-proof container. An old vitamin pill canister will do nicely, but keep it out of the reach of your pill-popping grandma! Do not risk exposing the seeds to any moisture as they could start to germinate before you are ready.

Proper seed storage in an airtight container is vital. Wrapping them in a plastic bag only results in moldy seeds and a waste of your money.

FEMINIZED SEEDS

As you might expect from the name, these seeds are more or less guaranteed to be female when grown in a stress-free environment. On the downside, they are more difficult to grow consistently and they tend to be more expensive than regular seeds. But on the positive side, you don't have to fret over the sex of your early flowering plant and risk misidentifying them, nor will you waste time, effort, or nutrients on male plants.

PREPARING TO GROW

Security

As cannabis cultivation is illegal, you should take pains to keep your green-fingered activity to yourself. Don't tell anyone that you don't *have to*. And certainly do not conduct guided tours of your grow room, however proud you might be of your massive buds. This is easier said than done as stoned people are generally not known for their discretion.

But it's not just loose lips that'll sink this particular ship. If you are using the same credit card to buy a bunch of "how to grow" books plus various seeds, lights, and a hydroponic kit, it will be pretty obvious to anyone monitoring transactions that there will shortly be more than just tomatoes sprouting in your greenhouse.

Similarly, if your electricity usage suddenly rockets in the height of summer, conclusions may be drawn. And innocent pleas of "I've been watching a whole lot of TV, man" (however truthful) will not cut it. I don't wanna make you any more paranoid than you already are, and clearly Big Brother isn't watching

everyone, despite what you might read, but growers have been caught for less.

And if the worst happens and the Feds discover your attic full of weed, you can always try claiming you were harvesting hemp to make a rope swing in your backyard.

That excuse will ring hollow as the cell door slams behind you, but on the flip side, you will have plenty of time to think of a better one for next time.

Be sensible with credit card use. Remember: just because you're paranoid doesn't mean they're not out to get you.

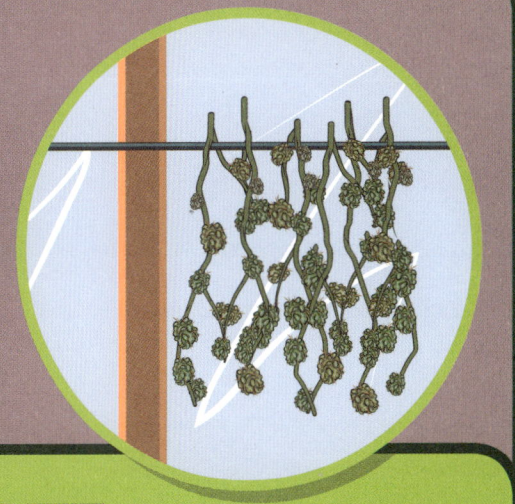

STAY PATIENT

As you've learned, the marijuana growth cycle can be a long and winding road. And you need to be on your guard throughout the process. It's not a lot of good taking multiple precautions through flowering and harvesting, only to dry your buds in front of the living room window for the world and his wife to see. Get wised up or you could get locked up. KnowwhatImean?

PREPARING TO GROW

Chapter 3: GROW-ROOM KIT AND SETUPS

"An acre of the best ground for hemp is to be selected and sewn in hemp and be kept for a permanent hemp patch."

—Thomas Jefferson's *Garden Book*, 1849

Now that you have decided where to grow, you need to understand the equipment you will need and your chosen method of cultivation (organic or hydroponic). Then it's time to guide you step by step through the process of creating your three classic garden setups. With that accomplished, you're ready for some serious action.

Indoor Materials And Set Up

Before you start thinking about setting up a grow room, let alone actually planting your first batch of weed, you need to understand the equipment you will need and the environmental preparations you need to make. As the old saying goes, failing to prepare means preparing to fail. Some items are more vital than others, some depend on the indoor-versus-outdoor environment, and some can be expensive, so here's the lowdown to help you keep it on the down low.

Light

It matters not whether you are growing sinsemilla, rose bushes, or apple trees—all plant life requires light in order to grow. Plants are nurtured via a process called *photosynthesis*. As you may remember from high school (if you weren't skipping class smoking reefers that day), photosynthesis is what plants have to do to live.

Essentially the term means "combining with light." It is the plant's means of generating food for itself from carbon dioxide and water. Simply put, if your plants don't get enough light, they won't photosynthesize and you'll have no buds.

With an outdoor grow, the sun takes care of business. Indoors, however, you need to provide your plants with artificial light. Your main options are described here.

Compact fluorescent lamps (CFLs)

Fluorescents are great for lighting the home and will happily get seedlings and cuttings to root, although experienced weed farmers will decry their ability to produce big buds. But for someone learning the ropes like yourself, they can do the job albeit with a reduced yield.

Envirolights are large CFLs specifically designed for horticultural use. They are available from all good grow stores and come in 125-watt and 200-watt sizes. The 125-watt bulb will set you back $45 (double the price for the 200-watt one), but that's just for the bulb. A basic reflector will cost as much again, so a reflector and two CFLs (one *blue* for vegetative growth and one *red* for flowering—see "Understanding spectrum" page 38) will cost around $135. If you're strapped for cash, you can get by with just the red bulb and use that for both stages.

High intensity discharge lamps (HIDs)

Most grow books recommend powerful metal halide or high pressure (HP) sodium lights—basically the same type that's used for street lighting. These are proven to produce the best yields, but here's the rub—at $200, they are far more expensive to buy than CFLs, and your electricity bill will contain more digits than you thought possible.

HID lights also require a ballast—a heavy electrical box that regulates the flow of current to the lamp. These babies create a lot of heat. If your grow space is restricted, like in a closet, it might make sense to locate the ballast outside of the closet. HIDs also produce much more heat than CFLs, so you may need to invest in a bigger extraction fan to keep the temperature down.

In summary, HIDs are expensive and complicated and best left for much later in your cultivation career.

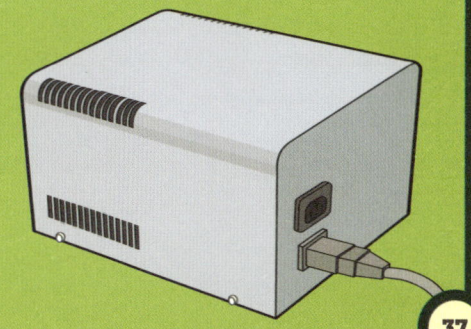

LET THERE BE LIGHT

As far as light goes, the more you use, the greater the yield (so long as it is the correct spectrum for the plants' growth stage).

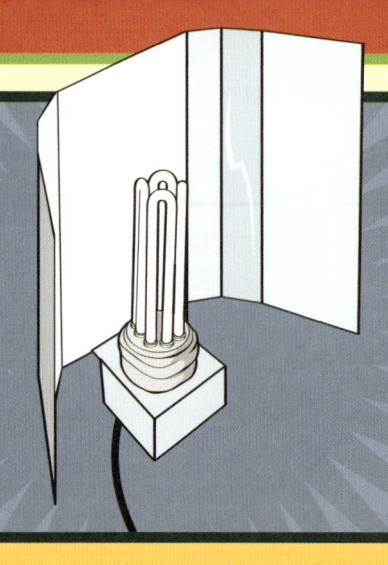

Reflectors
Usually forming part of the light you choose to buy, reflectors (canopies or hoods) reflect the light downward toward the plant(s). You can pick one up for about $45.

WINDOW GROW SPACE
If you wish, your indoor light can be outdoor light if you position your plants on the window ledge. Not only is this a potential security risk, though—it also means that you are reliant on the inconsistent power of the sun so will not derive any of the benefits of the indoor grow space.

Understanding spectrum
I won't blind you with science here, but light is categorized by color, or more specifically, *spectrum*. The *Kelvin scale* is the measure by which color in light is calculated for any type of horticulture. Cannabis grows well between 2,000 kelvin (red spectrum, for flowering) and 6,000 kelvin (blue spectrum, for vegetative growth). Check what spectrum your chosen lights operate at before you buy.

A word about wattages
The *wattage* is a measure of a lamp's power—the higher the wattage the brighter the light; it also indicates the amount of electricity it will consume; for example, a 250-watt light will consume 250 watts of electricity an hour. You can look at your electricity charge per kilowatt on your bill and calculate the cost.

Heat

Naturally produced by light, heat is also fundamental to cannabis growth. Cannabis is happiest at temperatures between 68°F and 82°F (20°C and 27°C). Although plants have been known to grow below 68°F, temperatures in excess of 86°F (30°C) will lead to a poor crop at best. Heat can be managed by the power of your lighting setup and extraction fans.

Humidity

This is the measure (expressed as a percentage) of water vapor in the air. As a rule of thumb, cannabis plants thrive in 50 percent humidity. If humidity levels reach 70 percent, your plants will be at risk of mold and other diseases (see chapter 7). As with heat, humidity levels can be managed with extraction fans.

Water

This is another essential requirement, of course. Plants need water for several reasons—it aids the absorption of minerals in the soil, helps the plant transport those minerals around its branches, is a key component of photosynthesis—and without it they wither and die. Plants should be moist at all times but not soaked. If the water is good enough for you to drink, it's fine for your garden.

Drainage

If your plants do not drain, they will quickly become waterlogged and die. Ensure that your planting pots have drainage holes. Place the pots on dishes or bowls to catch the excess water and avoid mess and empty them regularly.

Air

A good airflow is essential for any thriving garden. A supply of clean, fresh air brings your "babies" the carbon dioxide (CO_2) they need to photosynthesize and grow. In an outdoor environment Mother Nature takes care of business. But in an indoor grow room there are two issues. One, in a small confined space like a closet your air will very quickly go stale unless it is replaced, and two, there is no breeze to direct the air to all areas of the plant and to cool the heat from the lights. The grower needs two things to remedy this: ventilation and circulation fans.

Ventilation fan

Working on the same principle as a bathroom or kitchen fan, this will draw stale air out of the grow area and, at the flick of a switch, direct clean air in. Ideally, the fan will vent to an outside wall. Of course, making a hole in the wall of your property is not a job to be undertaken lightly. If such an installation is beyond your capabilities or budget, much the same effect could be

I'M YOUR SMALLEST FAN
Computer fans make for an ideal ventilation source for closet gardens. They are small, very easy to fit and wire up, and make very little noise.

achieved for free by opening the door of the grow box or closet for a period during daylight hours and blowing air in with a circulation fan. If you go with this method though, be sure to keep the window and door of the room open as much as possible to maximize ventilation.

Circulation fan

Not surprisingly, this circulates air around the grow room, replicating the effect of an outdoor breeze, which cools the plants, invigorates the leaves, helps to strengthen the branches, and ensures that air reaches every bit of the plant. A fan aimed directly at the light will help to cool the lamp and allow the light to be brought closer to the plant(s), increasing yields!

Odor control

This isn't about your personal hygiene, although that could probably do with some attention, but the smell given off by your pungent sinsemilla. This is only really an issue during the flowering phase when the resin is permeating everything with fragrant Eau de Weed. You'll love it, but others might not be so keen. This is a massive problem for commercial growers who must install carbon filters or ozone generators and plastic or metal ducting to dispel the strong waft of weed and prevent it from attracting the wrong kind of attention, but for a small grow project like yours, it shouldn't be an issue. At the simplest level, a few deodorizers in gel or spray form (which are commonly available) will do the trick.

GROW-ROOM KIT AND SETUPS

Pots

You can't grow pot plants without pots! Simple standard plastic pots from your local garden center will do. Use small ones (3 in. [7.6 cm]) for propagation and larger ones for vegetative and flowering growth. Make sure they are big enough, though. Some plants can grow many feet high, and if your pot's not big enough, the plant will become root-bound. Pots of the 3 gal. (11 L) size are commonly available at all good garden centers and are a popular choice to use from transplanting to harvest.

Space

A bit existential, this one, as it's not a tangible thing like lights or soil and may lead to some searching questions, like "Does space exist if you cannot see it?" If that's too much of a head trip for you, leave that debate for your next smoking session. For now, you just need to know it's important in a garden to allow your plants to grow and spread their branches uninhibited. A small closet with restricted height might be fine for the early stages of growth, but what are you gonna do when your plant doubles in size?

SEED TO WEED

Thermometer/hygrometer

Because cannabis thrives in a certain temperature and humidity range, you should invest in a thermometer/hygrometer, available at all grow shops and on the Web. It'll let you know the heat and humidity at all times, giving you a heads-up to change the ventilation settings as appropriate. Guessing the temperature from the heat on your hand isn't the same.

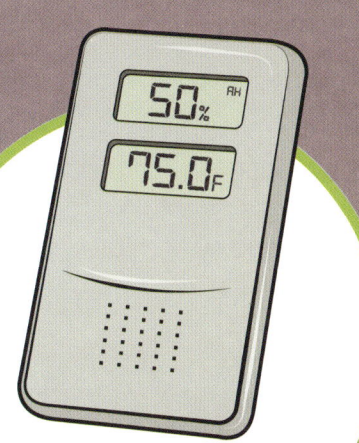

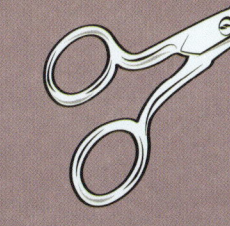

Magnifying glass

Act the super sleuth as you examine your plants for vital clues: at preflowering stage when you are searching for signs of sex; during late flowering when you are looking for signs of peak maturity; and at all times looking for indications of pest infestation—elementary, my dear pot grower. And when you're not busy doing all that, you can amaze yourself by looking at ordinary things through it while stoned (whoa, freaky).

Other odds and ends

There are several other items you'll need during your cultivation career, including some scissors, a small knife, and a syringe (for measuring out nutrients). None of these are particularly expensive and several can be "borrowed" from your grandma's greenhouse. She won't miss 'em.

How to set up an indoor box grow room

I use the term *box*, because this grow space could be one of several things—an old refrigerator, cupboard, packing case, closet, or wooden box you have constructed especially—in fact any structure with a door that roughly conforms to the dimensions given on page 23.

Here are the steps to setting up your box grow room.

You will need the following:

- *Paintbrush and white paint*
- *Mylar*
- *Waterproof sheeting*
- *Ventilation fan*
- *Circulation fan*
- *Lighting setup*
- *Thermometer/hygrometer*
- *Hammer and nails*
- *Drill*
- *Saw*
- *Screwdriver*

1

1 Clear the box of all existing contents; you may even discover that old bag of weed you thought you'd lost. Wash the area thoroughly with disinfectant and water. This may seem excessive, but fledgling plants are very vulnerable to disease. This is especially important if the area has previously been used for growing.

2 Paint the walls and ceiling with flat white paint or line them with Mylar (a thin reflective plastic sheeting developed by NASA, no less). This isn't vital, but it helps to direct light onto the plant(s) when they are *in situ*. Don't line the areas with aluminum foil because the heat can reflect with such intensity that it can burn holes through the leaves.

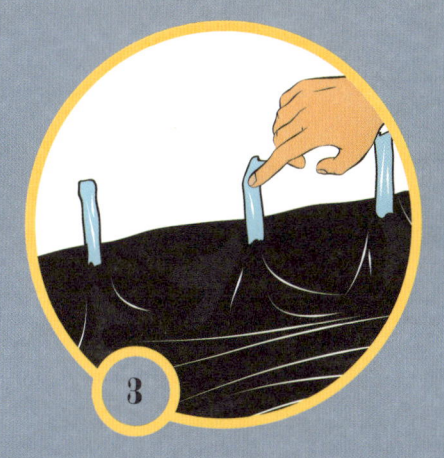

3 Cover the floor with waterproof sheeting to make the cleaning up of any spillage easier. Cut it slightly bigger than the floor size and tape or staple the overflow a few inches up the wall to ensure a good seal. If the floor is very cold, insulate it first or raise the plants off the floor.

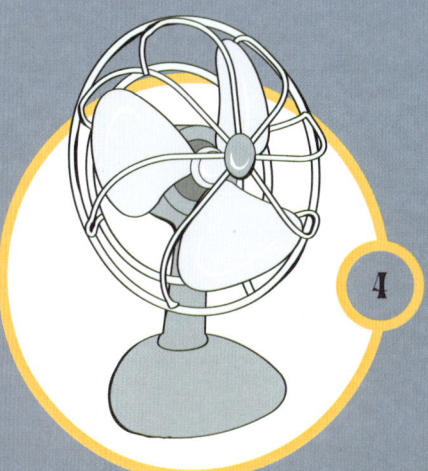

4 Place the circulation fan on a raised platform next to the plants. Cut a hole through the side of the box for the cable to reach the outside power source.

GROW-ROOM KIT AND SETUPS

5 Cut a hole in the wall of the box near to the ceiling to the exact size of your ventilation fan. Fix it in place and connect it to the power source. Either vent to an outside wall (seek professional help if you are at all fazed by this) or maximize ventilation in the room by keeping windows and doors open as much as possible.

6 Let there be light. Install your chosen light source, either fluorescent (CFL) or HID. Attach it to the ceiling of the box using screws, and hang it from adjustable chains or cords. It is important to be able to adjust the height of the lights to work around the plants as they increase in size.

GROW TENTS

These purpose-built pop-up grow rooms are available from all good grow stores. They take a lot of the hassle out of constructing a grow space, so if DIY ain't your thing, give one a try.

ELECTRICAL SAFETY

Sounds obvious but don't place electric items such as fans on the floor of your grow area where they may come into contact with water. Smoking cannabis won't kill you, but electricity can!

7 Link the lights to the ballast (if using HID) and also to a timer so your chosen photoperiod is managed automatically. Your memory is probably bad enough without adding the pressure of having to remember when to turn lights on and off manually.

8 Thermometer/hygrometer. Set this to the required level and simply hang it from a nail on the inside of the box. That way you will always be reminded to check both the temperature and humidity every time you open the door.

9 Bring on the plants! After a quick check to ensure all the electrical devices are working as they should, it's time to open the garden for business.

GROW-ROOM KIT AND SETUPS

47

Outdoor Materials And Set Up

In the controlled environment of the indoor grow room your actions are paramount. You determine the amount of water given to your plants and the levels of heat and humidity to which they are subjected. Outdoors, you are largely dependent on the whims of Mother Nature—your actions will have relatively little impact on the end result.

For instance, unless you've been stupid enough to plant your crop in the shadiest part of the garden, the light will take care of itself. Indeed, natural sunlight has the perfect spectrum for growing. And, depending on your location, some of your crop's water needs should fall from the sky.

Equipment

Some of the equipment applicable for the indoor grow, and already covered in detail, is apt for the outdoor environment as well. About all that can be added to the mix are standard legal gardening tools such as gardening gloves, a trowel, shovel, and fork, plus a pH tester/meter (see page 51).

How to set up a garden grow space

For the simplest and most natural garden setup, follow these rules for success every time. It's ironic after all the occasions your parents tried and failed to get you to help them do the gardening that you'll be embarking on this with such gusto.

1 Prepare early, ideally starting in the fall. Prior to planting, give the earth a good digging over, and remove any stones and large rooting systems.

2 Test the soil with your pH meter. Optimum soil for weed farming is between pH 6 and 7. If your soil is lower than pH 6 (too acidic), add some garden lime; if the reading is higher than pH 7 (too alkaline), add ground sulfur. If you are concerned about the suitability of your soil, purchase some loam (rich in nitrogen, lower in potassium and phosphorus). Add it to the area and fork it around and leave it for a few months to let nature take its course.

3 The following spring, clear the area of any weeds that have crept back. Then dig a hole (or holes) large enough to house the root ball of your seedling.

Greenhouse Grow Spaces

A combination of indoor and outdoor growing, greenhouses can be a good option. My tip would be to paint the walls white. Not only does this prevent anyone spying, but it will help reflect the light that comes in through the roof onto the plants.

GROW-ROOM KIT AND SETUPS

49

Organic Versus Hydroponic

The second key debate in cannabis cultivation circles centers on the style of growing medium to create your beautiful, bushy plants. The choice is between organic and hydroponics, essentially soil versus water. Both methods have their merits, and while you would never have a hydroponic grow outdoors, organic growing can be undertaken in either environment.

Some growers maintain that soil-grown weed is tastier than hydroponically grown pot, but I'm not sure about that. Organic setups do tend to be cheaper though—little more than the cost of some plastic pots and soil—whereas store-bought hydro setups with pH meters can cost from $300 upward. When perfected, hydro gardens do tend to produce bigger plants and higher yields in a shorter timeframe but the maintenance can be more fiddly than the traditional soil pot. As with the debate surrounding indoor or outdoor gardening, take a little time to decide what's right for you.

GARDEN SOIL
Don't just fill a pot with top soil from your backyard. This alone will not be suitable for growing prime bud. For more information about soil and other questions, consult your local garden center staff.

Organic

In a nutshell, organic growing is the traditional form that has served gardeners of all descriptions well for years. Basically, it involves putting soil in a pot, planting your seeds or seedling, and watering it regularly.

Soil

Standard potting soil is generally fine for growing marijuana. Pop to your local garden center to check out the range, but tell them you're growing tomatoes—anything but the truth—and stub that joint out first. Once you have engaged the assistant in conversation, the key things are to get soil that is fast-draining, has a neutral pH of 6–7 (see "pH tester/meter" on this page), and is high in nitrogen.

If you wanna get fancy, you can even create your own soil mix, a mind-blowing concoction built around varying percentages of perlite, compost, peat moss, worm castings, vermiculite, bark, top soil, and so on. Growers the world over swear by their own special ingredient balance, and the right mix can reap great rewards, but none of this'll matter a jot if you make basic errors such as overwatering your plants. Leave these soil shenanigans to the experts.

pH Tester/Meter

You might recall the term *pH*—the means of assessing the acidity or alkalinity of a solution—from chemistry classes in high school. The pH scale runs from 1–14, 1 being very acidic, 7 neutral, and 14 very alkaline. This might sound rather dull, but pH balance is very important in cannabis cultivation. Plants grow best (absorb nutrients most effectively) in soil or in a growing medium that has a neutral pH of 6–7. So a pH testing device is an essential tool to have at your disposal. Simply place the meter in the growing medium, and wait for the measurement to flash up.

If you discover your medium is too acidic, add some garden lime; if the reading is higher than pH 7 (too alkaline), add ground sulfur.

GROW-ROOM KIT AND SETUPS

51

Nutrients

NPK is a term you will hear a lot as you become immersed in the world of marijuana cultivation. It stands for nitrogen (N), phosphorus (P), and potassium (K), the primary ingredients for growth of marijuana or indeed any other plant. The *NPK ratio* represents the varying levels of these three nutrients present in growing mediums. Fickle plant that it is, cannabis has different nutritional requirements depending on its stage of the growth cycle.

N = green foliage

P = strong roots

K = healthy grow

Nitrogen, phosphorus, and potassium aren't the only nutrients your plants need. There's also magnesium (Mg), sulfur (S), iron (Fe), manganese (Mn), calcium (Ca), and more besides, but you needn't worry about these too much. After all, we're here to grow some bitchin' chronic, not learn the Periodic Table.

- For vegetative growth, the plant needs a food high in nitrogen so a suitable food will have an NPK of 15-5-5 or maybe 20-5-5 (the first figure is the "N" nitrogen content, so the higher the value, the more nitrogen it contains).

- Come flowering, the plant requires less nitrogen and more phosphorus in order to produce big buds so a suitable flowering food would have an NPK of around 10-30-10 (the second figure is the "P" content).

SEED TO WEED

52

Hydroponics

With hydroponic growing, the cannabis cultivator dispenses with soil and instead uses water (*hydro*, geddit?) and a growing medium that is inert. You may have heard the term *inert* before (referring to your state after a particularly potent reefer), but here it means chemically inactive, or having a neutral pH. This neutrality is important because all the nutrients the plants need are added to the water, which differs from organic growing.

Cannabis cultivators can choose from several inert mediums—foam rubber, gravel, lava chips, sand, rock wool, coir (a coconut fiber), and others. All of these feature good capillary action (an ability to absorb water—think of how water travels up a paper napkin), strong air-to-moisture ratios, and, of course, stable pH.

When it comes to getting the right nutrient solution, there's a bewildering choice of one-, two-, and three-part solutions available in hard- and soft-water varieties. As a beginner, you'll only really require two sets of nutrient solution—one for the *vegetative stage* (growth) and one for the *flowering stage* (bud production)—see chapter 4. To learn more about hydroponic growing mediums and nutrients, enquire at your local hydroponic store. Once you've bought your products, read the instructions carefully before applying.

Common hydro setups

Whereas the organic setup varies little beyond the soil-and-pot scenario, there are various methods by which to arrange your hydro setup. All options utilize a container filled with water and nutrient solution that is either *active* (pumped mechanically to the plants' roots) or *passive* (delivered nonmechanically). Here's a summary of the five most common setups.

Reservoir system (passive)

This is quite similar to organic in appearance. The plants sit in a large tray filled with water, and the roots are partly submerged. Depending on the size of your plot, these trays can be anything from an oven roasting pan to a children's paddling pool. (If using the latter, do the decent thing and buy little Johnny a replacement!) The bottom half of each pot is filled with clay pellets that absorb the nutrient-rich water through capillary action. Some conventional gardening experts maintain that it is unhealthy for the plant's roots to be in direct contact with water. If you're concerned by this, there's always the wick system.

Wick system (passive)

This is similar to the reservoir system, but the water is drawn from the tray into the bottom of the pots by a nylon cord (wick). The pots are positioned on raised blocks, out of the water, and the wick dangles down into the reservoir. Both the wick and reservoir systems are suitable for first-time growers.

Wick system

Wick in contact with water

Air pump oxygenates the nutrient solution

Ebb and flow (active)

Also called the *flood*, this approach is a little more complicated and expensive. This time the tray is more of a waterproof table with side walls. Water is transferred to the table from a nearby reservoir via an electrically powered pump. Once the water reaches a certain level and is irrigating the plants, it automatically starts to drain back into the reservoir. Store-bought kits contain the tray, a reservoir, a planting unit, timer, pump, and pump tubing . . . or you can build your own.

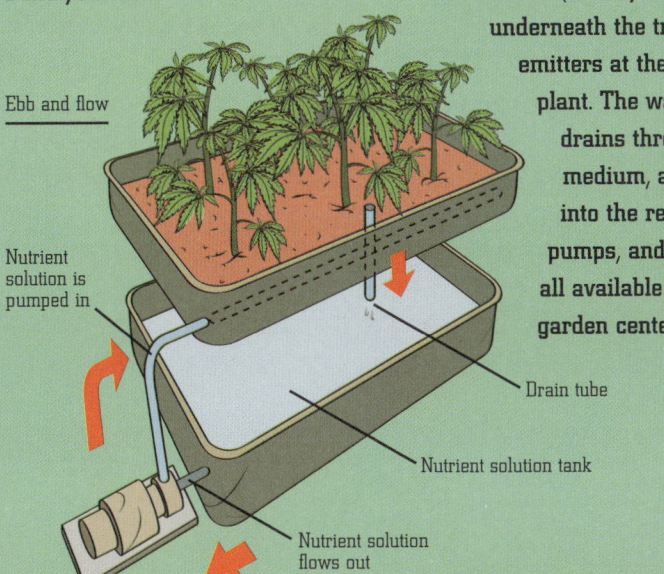

Ebb and flow

Nutrient solution is pumped in

Drain tube

Nutrient solution tank

Nutrient solution flows out

Drip (active)

Again, this is a twist on a common theme. This time the water and nutrients are delivered to the top rather than to the bottom of the plants. A pump system transfers water from a reservoir (usually located underneath the tray) to special emitters at the top of each plant. The water flows out, drains through the medium, and goes back into the reservoir. Tubing, pumps, and emitters are all available at regular garden centers.

Nutrient film technique (NFT) (active)

This system is based around the theory that marijuana (indeed many other legal) plants thrive when their roots are exposed to a constant flow of nutrient-rich water. By spraying water onto or flowing water over the roots, they are in contact with a continual film of nutrients. The simplest way of setting this up is to prepare a standard drip system and fill the pots with pebbles. With the drippers permanently on, a thin film of water will attach to the pebbles. There are more complex versions of this that can be bought.

At its best, NFT works extremely well, but it does require great care and attention to ensure all the emitters are working at all times. This method is an unnecessary headache for the first-time grower.

GROW-ROOM KIT AND SETUPS

Building a homemade bubbler

The good news is that it's not necessary to use store-bought hydroponic setups if you're only growing a couple of plants. The homemade bubbler works by sending air through a tube into the nutrient solution. An air stone (which diffuses oxygen) inside the container bubbles water at the surface, which splashes the roots of your seedlings. Follow these instructions to build a trouble-free homemade bubbler.

1 Place the nets on top of the lid and trace around them with the marker pen.

2 Cut the holes slightly inside the lines you have marked and place the nets into the lid so the net tops catch on the lid and prevent them from falling in.

You will need these materials to follow the instructions here:

- 3 gal. (11 L) plastic container with lid
- Water-resistant adhesive
- Marker pen
- Scissors and sharp knife
- Plastic net pots (two)
- Fish-tank air pump
- Length of plastic air tubing (4 ft. [120 cm])
- One-way check valve
- Air stone
- Drill
- White plastic sheeting

3 Pierce or drill a hole (1/5 in. [5 mm]) in one side of the container a couple of inches up from the bottom.

4 Insert the valve into the hole and use water-resistant adhesive to secure it in place. Cut off a small piece of the air tubing.

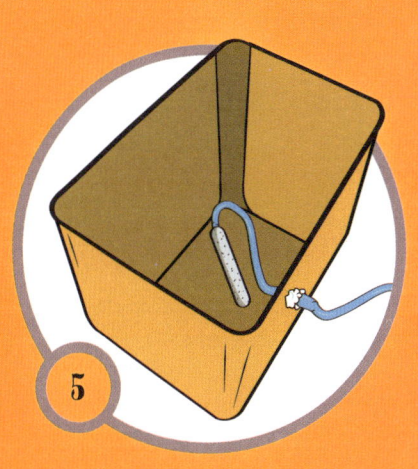

5 Insert one end into the valve on the inside of the container. Attach the other end to the air stone.

6 Insert the remaining air tube into the valve on the outside of the container and attach the other end to the fish-tank pump.

GROW-ROOM KIT AND SETUPS

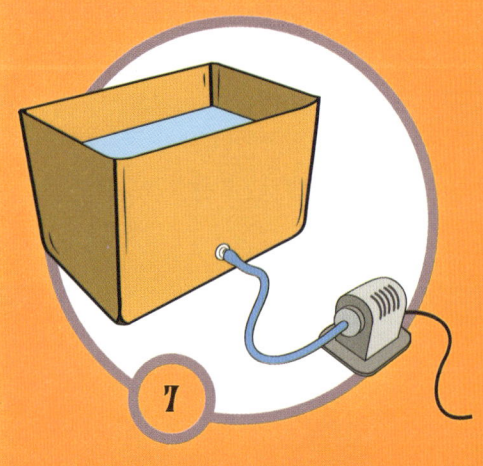

7 Fill the container with your mix of water and nutrient solution so it just covers the bottom of the net pots when the lid's in place.

8 Assemble your growing medium—rock wool, clay pebbles, and so on—and run the pump for twenty-four hours.

9 The following day, transplant your seedlings into the net pots and add more growing medium to support the plants. Lower the pots into the holes in the bubbler lid.

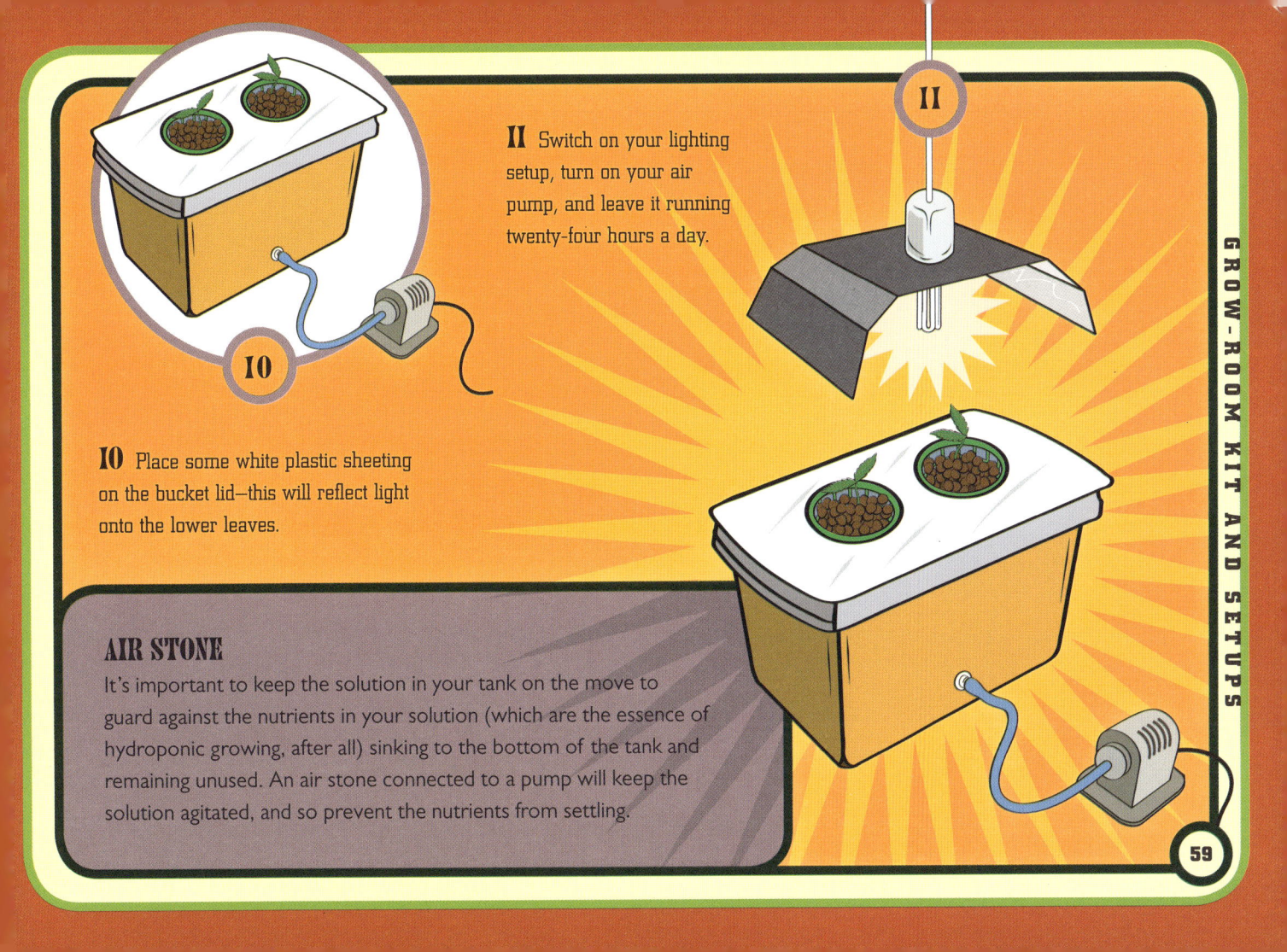

11 Switch on your lighting setup, turn on your air pump, and leave it running twenty-four hours a day.

10 Place some white plastic sheeting on the bucket lid—this will reflect light onto the lower leaves.

AIR STONE

It's important to keep the solution in your tank on the move to guard against the nutrients in your solution (which are the essence of hydroponic growing, after all) sinking to the bottom of the tank and remaining unused. An air stone connected to a pump will keep the solution agitated, and so prevent the nutrients from settling.

GROW-ROOM KIT AND SETUPS

chapter 4
LET'S GET GROWING

"Give a friend a bud and you'll get them high for a day; teach a friend to grow and you'll get them high for life."

—Jeff Ditchfield, grower and founder of Bud Buddies

Now that you know the basics of marijuana cultivation, it's time to give those green fingers some practice. Like a mother with a newborn child, your focus for the next couple of months will be nurturing your offspring to full maturity. But in return, you will get the sweet smell of sinsemilla rather than sleepless nights and dirty diapers.

Germination

This is where the adventure begins. With due care and attention your seeds will soon show the first signs of life. For seeds to germinate they require moisture, heat, and air.

Moisture

Seeds contain about 20 percent moisture naturally. When this is raised to around 80 percent, germination begins. A seed needs moisture at two stages in its early life. First, to penetrate the shell (*testa*) and allow the root to emerge. (This shell-splitting can also be achieved with heat, but water is more reliable in my opinion.) Then, once growth has started, moisture is required to transport nutrients, hormones, and so on to promote further development.

Heat

Evidence suggests that seeds flourish best at temperatures around 75°F–80°F (24°C–26.5°C). If the temperature is below 70°F (21°C), germination will probably be slowed and may not occur at all; above 90°F (32°C) and there'll be growth irregularities.

Air (oxygen)

Overwatering your seeds is a common mistake made by first-time growers as is planting the seeds too deeply in the planting mix. Both these errors will restrict the air supply to the seed.

Save Your Seeds

My advice would be to germinate only half your seeds at a time. That way, if it all goes horribly wrong, at least you won't have wasted the whole packet.

Step-by-step towel propagation

Seeds are usually germinated by paper towel or cheesecloth propagation. A grower's favorite, this is inexpensive and more reliable than soil germination. After all, it worked when you grew watercress in high school! The seeds cannot grow into plants in this environment but must be transferred to soil or propagation kits once the root has broken through. But they gotta start somewhere.

1 Soak the seeds in a glass of water (to break down the casing) for no more than twenty-four hours. If the water quality in your areas is poor, boil it and allow to cool before soaking the seeds. At first, the seeds will float, but as they grow heavier with the penetration of the water they will sink. One or two of the seeds may already show the first part of the root.

SEEDLINGS ARE GRATE

To save you the worry of your seeds becoming swamped, use a container with drainage holes rather than a dinner plate.

2 Set out an ordinary dinner plate and place some paper towels or cheesecloth on it. Slowly add some fresh water until saturated.

LET'S GET GROWING

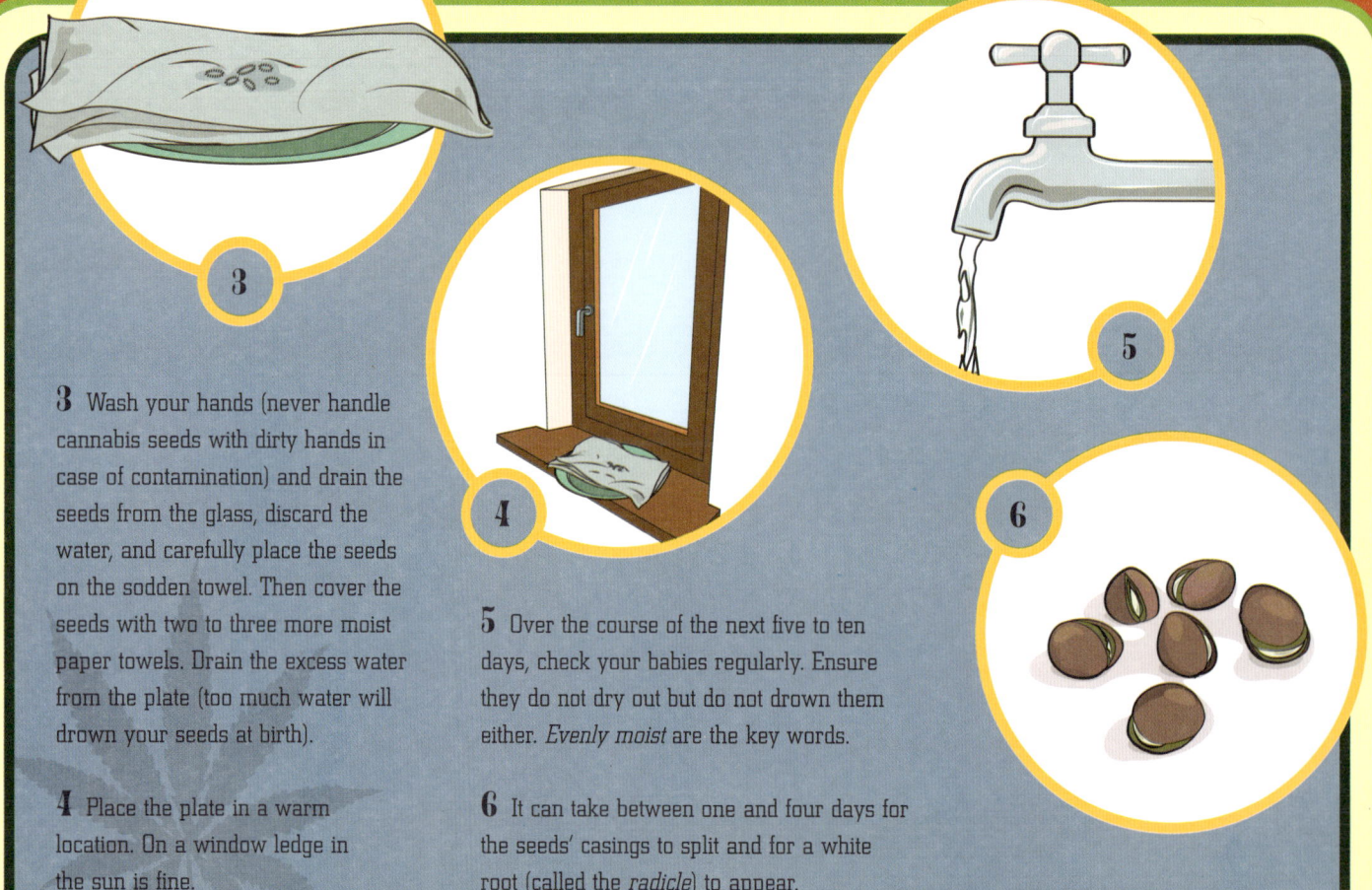

3 Wash your hands (never handle cannabis seeds with dirty hands in case of contamination) and drain the seeds from the glass, discard the water, and carefully place the seeds on the sodden towel. Then cover the seeds with two to three more moist paper towels. Drain the excess water from the plate (too much water will drown your seeds at birth).

4 Place the plate in a warm location. On a window ledge in the sun is fine.

5 Over the course of the next five to ten days, check your babies regularly. Ensure they do not dry out but do not drown them either. *Evenly moist* are the key words.

6 It can take between one and four days for the seeds' casings to split and for a white root (called the *radicle*) to appear.

Propagation

When the radicles have grown to around three times the length of the seed, they are ready to be transplanted into your chosen growing medium and begin the next stage of their cycle, which takes place in a *propagator*.

A propagator is a simple device that's available from all good garden centers. It consists of a heated mat and clear plastic lid. This warm, damp environment allows freshly germinated seeds to flourish. The propagator should be placed under a low-wattage light or on a windowsill. Propagation can take place either organically or hydroponically.

DIY PROPAGATOR

You can improvise your own propagator using a tray covered with an inverted Tupperware box, then placing it in a warm location.

LET'S GET GROWING

Soil propagation

Seeds are placed a few millimeters below the surface of the soil and kept moist by watering daily. This method is probably not ideal for the first-time grower although special soils exist (high in nitrogen and containing a blend of nutrients) that increase your chances of success.

1 Obtain a seed flat (available from all grow shops and garden centers).

2 Fill it with specialist soil and make a small hole in the soil of each compartment with the end of a pen. This is the hole in which your seed will live; do not make the hole any more than twice the length of the seed. At this age, the seeds do not have enough energy to burst through the soil for sprouting, so to bury them too deep would be to kill them off.

Feminize your seeds

If you don't have specially-bought feminized seeds it's still possible to alter a seed's gender by soaking it in a solution containing estrogen, a female hormone. Dissolve a female contraceptive pill in some warm water, pop the seeds in and leave overnight. If you're male and your wife or girlfriend doesn't have the Pill, it's probably unwise to seek a prescription from your doctor. . . .

3 Carefully move your seeds (one at a time) to the seed flat by gently gripping the seed casing, never the root, with some tweezers. Place each seed in its allocated hole, ensuring that the root is facing downward.

4 Cover the seed with a thin layer of soil and very gently press it into place.

5 Place the seed flat in the propagator and turn on the heating mat.

LET'S GET GROWING

Hydroponic propagation

Two of the most popular mediums to use are rock wool cubes and Oasis pots. Rock wool is a mixture of melted rock and sand that is spun into thread and compressed. Oasis is a foam with similar properties. Both are sterile, nondegradable, and very porous, meaning the roots receive plenty of nutrients and air.

If using one of these specialist growing mediums, you should consult the product's instructions. Essentially though, follow these rules.

1 Fill the bottom of the tray with nutrient-rich solution (see page 53).

2 Place the grow cubes in the slots provided so that part of the cube is in contact with the solution.

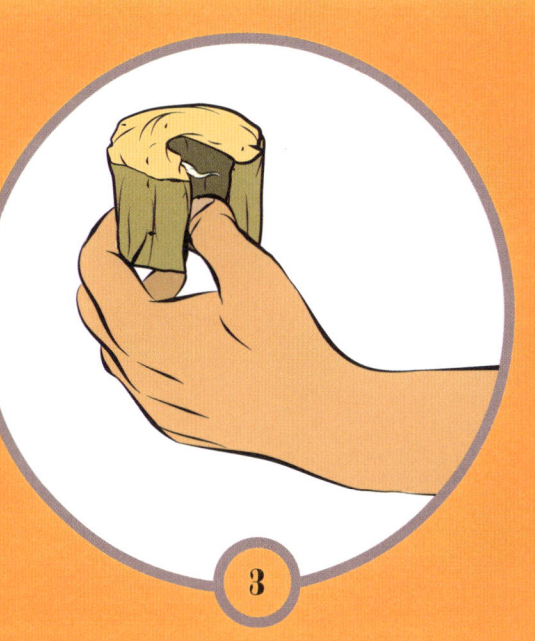

3 Place the seeds in the holes provided, replace the lid, and turn on the heating mat. Provided you keep the solution topped up, nature should take care of it.

LET'S GET GROWING

Growth progress

The growth of your seedlings will now follow of the same course through to transplanting, irrespective of your chosen method of propagation.

Preparation

A good tip to help maximize propagation success is to presoak the medium in a 50 percent strength nutrient solution for twenty-four hours, then to give the cubes a gentle squeeze to expel excess solution before adding the seed.

1 After six days of careful daily watering and maintenance of temperature, your patience should be rewarded: there should be clear signs of growth above the soil line or out of the rooting cube. After a further few days, the seedling will be displaying embryonic leaves (known as the cotyledon).

2 Within two weeks of your initial towel germination, if all has gone according to plan your seeds should be displaying several "classic" cannabis leaves—that is, serrations with pointed tips. If your young plants don't look like this, you may have got your seeds mixed up with your granny's tomato seeds. Doh! This will be greatly disappointing for you but nothing compared with the major surprise it will be for ol' granny.

AFTERCARE

Your young seedlings need a little TLC in the days immediately after propagation. By all means, move them into the grow room if you are using one, but for the first seven to ten days, until the plants have developed a healthy root system and grown at least three sets of true leaves, you should keep the lights at fairly low intensity—a 125-watt (blue/white) CFL is ideal. Don't have it too close to the plants, either; 18–24 in. (45–60 cm) above the tops of the plants is about right.

LET'S GET GROWING

Transplanting

Your plants are almost ready to enter a rapid stage of growth. However, to facilitate this for indoor growing, you'll need to move the plants to larger pots, known as *transplanting*. Depending on your strain, your plant may reach heights of 7 ft. (2 m), something it is clearly incapable of doing while there is only space for its roots to expand a few inches. Transplanting is done like this.

I Prepare a new, larger container by filling it about two-thirds full with loam soil (or any soil high in nitrogen with a neutral pH).

Which Pot?

Although plant size depends on strain, generally the bigger the pot you choose, the larger your plant can grow. The choice you make depends on the space you have available and the amount of buds you wish to grow. For most indoor small-scale grows, a 2½–4 gal. (10–15 L) pot is plenty.

SEED TO WEED

2 Use a knife to work away at the sides of your soil flat or rooting cube to separate it from its container. This may take some time. Do not rush this process or try to force the seedling out as that could damage its roots.

3 When it is dislodged, tip the plant out and hold it by the soil base. Some soil will probably fall away during this process, but this does not matter. Do not hold the seedling by its top leaves (they will come away in your hand, dumbass); don't hold it by the stem either, as this can cause other damage.

LET'S GET GROWING

4 Place the root ball in the new container, add extra soil to cover the base, and gently pat the soil down.

5 If possible, place your plants on blocks above the tray so the bottom of the pot does not come into contact with any water that has drained out of it.

DRYING OUT

A useful tip is not to water the seedling the day before transplanting. If the soil is dry, it will be easier to remove the seedling from its original container.

Outdoor transplanting

If you are planning to grow marijuana in pots on your patio then the same process of transplanting applies. However, if you intend to plant into the outdoor garden then now is the time. Planting out should occur in the spring, after any lingering frost has cleared, certainly by mid to late April.

1 Remove your seedlings carefully from their rooting cubes as described on the previous page and place in the holes you dug in your outdoor grow space (see page 49). Gently cover the root ball over with soil and water.

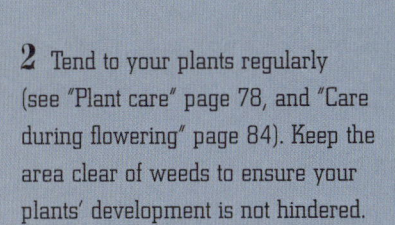

2 Tend to your plants regularly (see "Plant care" page 78, and "Care during flowering" page 84). Keep the area clear of weeds to ensure your plants' development is not hindered.

LET'S GET GROWING

Vegetative Growth

Now is the time to really kick some ass in the growing cycle. The vegetative stage is defined by rapid growth (up to an inch a day in healthy plants). But this won't happen on its own, at least not at the breakneck speed you want.

Light and dark

You need to put your seedlings in your grow room and expose them to eighteen to twenty-four hours of light per day. The more light they receive, the faster they will grow, so continual light is often considered best, providing your budget allows it.

However, many growers believe that a period of six to eight hours of darkness per day results in a greater percentage of females in the garden, as well as being easier on the wallet. You decide!

These photoperiods are commonly abbreviated as 18/6 (eighteen hours of light, six of darkness) and 24/0 (twenty-four hours of light).

Photoperiod:
18/6 or 24/0

Temperature:
70°F–75°F (21°C–24°C)

Humidity:
50–60 percent

pH:
6–7, slightly acidic or neutral

How long:
Two to four weeks

Heat

Increase the intensity of your lighting setup to 500-watt envirolight and lower the lights so they give as much light to the plant tops as possible without burning the leaves. This action will give your plants the maximum power available from your light, and it will encourage vigorous vegetative growth. Remember the Kelvin scale from chapter 3? You will need a blue light emitting at about 6,000 kelvin for the vegetative growth stage.

You should aim to mirror the optimum temperatures for outdoor growing inside. This is 75°F (24°C) during the day and 65°F–70°F (18°C–21°C) at night and humidity of 60 percent. You can manage the levels of heat reaching your plants by adjusting the height of your lights (or that of your plants by standing them on a raised platform such as an empty plastic container). Humidity can be controlled by an extraction fan. If humidity drops below 50 percent, you can raise the level by hanging a wet dish towel in the grow box.

Right Height

As a rule of thumb, the light is the correct height when you are able to hold your hand under the heat at the plant's height for thirty seconds or so without undue distress.

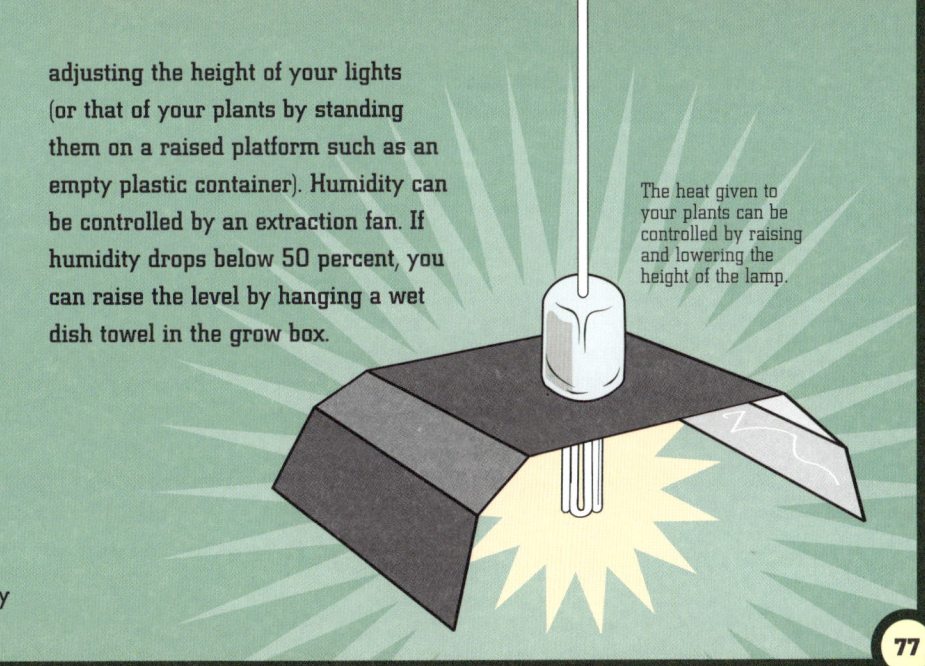

The heat given to your plants can be controlled by raising and lowering the height of the lamp.

LET'S GET GROWING

Plant care

Of course, light alone will not make your garden grow. You will need to water and fertilize your plants as well as provide a clean flow of air. You can underwater and underfertilize as easily as giving excessive doses, so check out the information about your strain.

The plants should be watered when the soil begins to show signs of drying at about an inch below the surface. Typically this will be every three to four days. At each watering, the plants should be fed with fertilizer. Choose a water-soluble fertilizer from your local garden center. Miracle-Gro, Dyna-Gro, Formula Flora, and organic fertilizers such as bat guano (that's bat poo!) work fine. Not all cannabis strains are the same, so fertilize accordingly. In general, sativas require less fertilizer than indicas. Beware that over-fertilization can be more harmful to your crop than growing in poor soil with inadequate lighting.

Typically, plants should be left in the vegetative growth stage for about four to five weeks or until they are 12–18 in. (30–45 cm) tall. However, a plant can only flourish to a size its pot allows. For a 6 in. (15 cm) diameter pot, the vegetative stage might only last two weeks.

The plants require plenty of nitrogen during this period to promote green leafy growth. But if the plants become too tall, that leafy growth will inhibit the light from reaching the lower branches and be counterproductive. If you're thinking this all sounds a bit trial and error—you'd be right. As with many facets of cannabis production, there is no substitute for practice.

WATCH THE BUDGET
If you blithely keep the lights on with no thought to cost, you will get a nasty shock, which only a large joint will temper, when the electricity bill lands on your doormat. So beware.

Hydro care

If you are growing hydroponically, plant care during the vegetative stage is much the same as if you are growing in soil. Enrich the water using a special hydroponic fertilizer, paying close attention to the product's instructions. Try brands such as Technaflora, VitaMax™, and General Hydroponics. The pH should be balanced at 6–7, and the water in the hydro setup should be changed completely every week.

Stay-at-home parent

Now that you have a garden underway, you need to show dedication to the cause. Just as the farmer is bound to a field of crops, so you must tend to your plants and avoid any extended absences. So that means no vacations during the growth cycle and certainly no palming off the responsibility on others. While it's okay to ask the next-door neighbor to feed your goldfish and water your roses while you're away on vacation, getting that neighbor to prune your closet full of marijuana is an imposition too far!

Preflowering

During the vegetative stage the plants will quickly develop new leaves and the stem will become thicker but the growth in these early days will be fairly vertical. After a couple of weeks, however, providing your plant is happy and healthy, it will start what is known as *secondary* or *lateral* branching. Basically, it will start bushing out. The first signs of this will be evidence of growth at the *nodes* (the minuscule area between the stem and branch offshoot). These growths produce new leaves, then branches, and eventually flowers.

Over the coming weeks the plant will become bushier and these node regions will multiply. After four to eight weeks following germination, depending on strain (some sativas may take even longer), the plant should be ready to show its sex (that is, grow flowers in the interests of reproduction).

Spotting the Sex

Now take a couple of deep breaths, not a spliff break, and pay attention because this next bit is a little complicated—but it's vital. Experienced growers will be able to tell with the naked eye at a very early stage the sex of their individual plants. You, on the other hand, will think your six-week-old plant looks the same as it did ten days ago, but it may not be, which is why a magnifying glass is

Force Flower

If you are still unsure of the sex (you really are paranoid, aren't you!), you can always take a cutting, put it in some rock wool as you would with a clone (see chapter 6), and force it to flower by exposing it to 12/12 (twelve hours of light, twelve hours of darkness). If you still can't tell after that, you should try another hobby.

Male

Male preflowers
(*staminate primordia*)

Female

Female pistils and calyx
(*pistillate primordia*)

a vital tool. As discussed on page 18, it is crucial you identify the male plants in your crop at the earliest opportunity so they can be culled. You are searching for what is called *calyx development*. I don't expect you to remember that and it doesn't matter so long as you know what it looks like, but the calyx is the layer that protects a flower in bud. If the calyx is raised on a short stem, it is a male; if it is unraised, it is a female.

At a slightly later stage of development, and to be extra sure (since you don't want to cull a garden full of aspiring sinsemilla because of your rampant paranoia about male flowers), the flowers of either sex will look like this: male flowers will develop into small miniature grape-like balls; female flowers will not be spherical and will have hairs (*pistils*) growing from the top.

If your male flowers look like this (see below), which can occur as soon as twenty-four to forty-eight hours after initial calyx development, you are probably too late. The pollen sack has opened, and those wanton females will be lapping it up.

An open male pollen sack will mean mayhem in your garden.

LET'S GET GROWING

81

Photoperiod:

12/12

Temperature:

70°F–75°F (21°C–24°C)

Humidity:

60 percent (50 percent during late flowering)

pH:

6–7

How long:

Approximately eight weeks

Flowering

Once you have identified the plant's sex and removed any males from the garden, the sinsemilla is ready for flowering. If you are growing indoors, it is your decision whether you do that or not. Many indoor cannabis plants will happily stay in the vegetative stage of their life for a decade or more (see "Mother Plant" in chapter 6), continuing to develop nodes, more leaves, and branches. There are advantages to this—the more nodes the plant has, the greater the opportunities for flowers, meaning juicy buds, but a lot depends on the plant's genetics and its growing conditions as to whether this comes to pass.

However, there are three big downers about maintaining vegetative growth.

1 The plants are prone to stress-related problems.

2 Every week you leave it is another week on the overall schedule, which is not good if you're in a hurry for a decent smoke.

3 And the plant will continue to grow . . . and grow. Before you know it, it'll be like *Day of the Triffids*.

12/12

Not as "down with the kids" as the phrase 24/7, but 12/12 is one of the most significant principles in cannabis cultivation. Indoor marijuana plants don't decide to flower on their own. This process is not triggered by age nor by a full moon, leap years, or any other crazy notion you may have. It is purely down to the amount of light the plants receive in each twenty-four-hour period—determined by the onset of fall in the wild but manipulated artificially by the cannabis cultivator indoors. When your 18/6 or 24/0 setup is changed to 12/12 (twelve hours of light and twelve hours of darkness), your plants will flower, whether they are 6 in. or 6 m tall.

WHERE IN THE WORLD?

Of course, the seasons are not the same all over the world, varying according to latitude. On the 44th parallel, which bisects New York, the day length is approximately sixteen hours in June, falling to nine hours in December, with flowering occurring naturally near the end of September. In the equivalent southern parallel, which bisects New Zealand, the hours are the same but the seasons reversed. So flowering will occur at the end of March (the start of their fall). The nearer to the equator you live, the less drastic the change in photoperiod—on the equator the day length is approximately twelve hours in June and eleven hours in December. Not a lot of people know that. . . .

Care during flowering

Once your sinsemilla enters 12/12, it is imperative that the lighting regimen is adhered to. It's no good opening the closet door to check on their well-being, however well intentioned. When it's dark it needs to stay dark. Your garden needs to be lightproofed. This can be as simple as draping a dark sheet over your box grow space.

You should change your lighting setup for the flowering stage, as bud production rather than rapid growth is now your focus. Opt for a lamp in the red spectrum, at around 2,700 kelvin, and again get it as close to the tops of the plants as you can.

Less water intake is usually required than in the vegetative stage (beware the dangers of overwatering), and the plants forsake nitrogen (needed for leaf growth) for higher levels of potassium and phosphorus (which stimulate flower development). To reflect this change of emphasis in the plant's needs, many fertilizer manufacturers offer a "bloom" version of their product, which should be used at this stage of the growth process.

Early flowering

Of course, you can control the flowering of your plant, certainly with indoor growing, so, in theory, by changing the photoperiod you can put a plant into flower at any point if you have used feminized seeds, even at 6 in. tall. Naturally, the shorter the plant at the time, the less mature it will be and the less bud it will be able to carry. So for an optimum yield, you should wait until preflowering and the plant shows its sex. Failure to do so will probably lead to stress-related sex problems (hermaphrodites) and abnormal bud growth.

Pruning, Staking, And Training

As your plants grow taller and develop (hopefully) weighty buds, they may require some assistance from your green thumbs to facilitate optimum growth and yield. As with any plant with numerous branches and flowers, the tallest compete for the light. If your plants are left untouched, they can grow at undesirable angles, the leaves and buds on the higher branches can block the light to those lower down the stem, and the branches can droop with the weight of the buds. To direct the plant's energy most efficiently, it is sometimes better to cultivate a smaller number of buds to a large size than many buds at smaller sizes. This is where you come in.

Step-by-Step Pruning and Staking

Typically plants should be pruned a couple of times during the flowering stage, first, a few days after the 12/12 photoperiod is started and again about a fortnight (two weeks) later. Large fan leaves that are blocking light from reaching the buds should be trimmed at all times.

You will need scissors or clippers, bamboo stakes, and plastic twist ties.

1 Identify the four or five thickest branches on your plant, spaced evenly.

2 Cut away the other weaker branches. Sever them at a 45° angle at the node. Now trim the larger leaves from your remaining branches. Your plant should now resemble a classic tree shape.

3 Insert bamboo stakes into the soil at different points around the pot's circumference, one for each of these larger branches.

4 Carefully tie the middle of each branch to the stake. Voilà, you have a carefully pruned plant ready to deliver maximum bud growth.

SEED TO WEED

Training

Although you don't want to cause your crop undue stress, the stems of plants are flexible and can be bent in various ways to best fit your space. For instance, if height is an issue in your grow area, you can train your plants to grow horizontally. Simply tie some string to the top part of the stem and attach the other end to the side of the grow box. (Or, tie the tops of the plants to a wooden frame, as shown.) Tighten the string daily until the plant has learned what you want it to do. Cannabis plants are surprisingly quick on the uptake . . . certainly sharper than you. If the plants in your outdoor grow space are becoming scarily tall ("I'm sure it said *indica* on the seed packet . . . "), you can wrap twine around the upper part of the main stem, bend the plant over, and secure it with pegs hammered into the earth.

LET'S GET GROWING

Stages Of Flowering

As the female plants develop, the calyxes become more dense, forming clusters at the node points along the stem. Such clusters are known as *colas*. As maturity increases (usually about halfway through the flowering period), the plant will start to show white crystals, almost as if covered in a sticky fine sugar.

Don't worry, this is not an infestation; it's actually a very good thing. As can be seen with a magnifying glass, these crystals are minute hairs that grow from the pistils. These are the trichomes described earlier, and they contain the THC-rich resin you crave. They are sticky because they are looking to trap any male pollen that is in the air—which of course they won't do so long as you've done as instructed!

There are many pistils, but far too few buds are in development.

As the trichomes wither and die (and are replaced by new ones) the resin falls onto other areas of the bud and surrounding leaves. So, as the plant reaches peak maturity (anywhere between seven and twelve weeks) much of the plant will have a frosted look and pistils that are a mainly yellow/brown in color. When you can see very few green pistils it means

early flowering

the plant has more or less given up its search for male pollen. And you know what that means? After weeks of displaying patience you never knew you had, it's harvest time!

Pistils are now starting to turn brown, but this flower still has a couple of weeks to run.

middle flowering

late flowering

Harvest now. Trichomes degrade rapidly from this point.

POT PORN
For some truly awesome pictures of buds up close and personal, get Jason King's *Cannabible*.

LET'S GET GROWING

89

Growing Timeline

Day 1
Put seeds in water.

Day 2–5
Germinate on towel or cheesecloth.

Day 5–6
Transfer to growing medium; see immediate signs of growth.

Day 7–10
Seedlings show cotyledon leaves.

Day 10–14
Seedlings show true (serrated and pointed) cannabis leaves.

SEED TO WEED

Day 22–30
Grow your seedlings under fluorescent light for seven to ten days and pay close attention to them.

Day 32+
Once they have developed a good root structure, they are ready to enter the vegetative stage. This can last from fourteen days to eight weeks.

Day 31
Transplant the seedlings that are ready for vegetative growth.

Day 14–21
Keep the soil evenly moist.

When your plants are at the size you want, change the lighting regime to 12/12 and start to feed them with a flowering food. The total amount of time in flower will depend on the strain you are growing; an indica variety can be ready to harvest after as little as fifty-six days of flower; a sativa variety could take up to twenty weeks.

LET'S GET GROWING

chapter 5
HARVESTING AND CURING

"Marijuana, in its natural form, is one of the safest therapeutically active substances known to man."

—DEA Chief Administrative Law Judge Francis L. Young, 1988

Harvesting is a time of joy for any cannabis connoisseur. After remaining patient for many weeks, if not months, the time has finally arrived when you can prepare your bud for smoking. In the immortal words of Lou Reed, "You're going to reap just what you sow." It certainly will be a Perfect Day when you pick those buds!

HARVESTING AND CURING

When To Harvest

Essentially the time to harvest is when the plant's buds have all matured and THC levels have reached maximum for that strain. The novice grower like yourself should be looking for buds that feature yellow/brown pistils and frosted leaves (as noted earlier). This could be anywhere between seven to twelve weeks depending on the strain. Watch for the following indicators:

- Around two-thirds of the pistils have turned yellow/brown—they are withering and dying because they are no longer needed to gather pollen, but this is good!

- The plants have stopped producing crystals (trichomes) and resin, and the buds are not growing appreciably.

- The larger leaves have yellowed and are falling off.

With an early harvest you are simply robbing yourself of the best smoke. Resin development will be lower and therefore so will THC content. If your buds look predominately white/pale green/yellow they are far from peak. It pays to wait. Wait too long though (buds are predominately red/brown) and levels of CBN rise relative to THC. In laymen's terms this means you will generally experience a couch-locked high irrespective of whether you harvested indica or sativa.

SAMPLE YOUR WARES

Another, and frankly more enjoyable, way to gauge if your weed is ready is to smoke a bit. Pick a small piece of bud from the flowering plant, wrap it in some tissue paper and place it on a sunny windowsill for a couple of hours (or in a microwave, minus the paper, on low heat for a couple of minutes).

When the bud is dry and brittle, spark it up. This extreme drying process will result in a harsh smoke and will have destroyed some of the THC, but you should still get a decent hit from it. If not, you have probably acted too early and need the plant to flower some more.

THE BIGGER PICTURE!

Use the magnifying glass you had for identifying the sex to get a better appreciation of the pistils and trichomes and understand the optimum time for harvest.

PREHARVEST TIPS

Do not water the plants for twenty-four to forty-eight hours before harvest. This will dry the buds out a little before they are cut. Also, subject the grow room to forty-eight hours of complete darkness. This will encourage more resin to develop. More resin means a better smoke!

HARVESTING AND CURING

Harvest Time

So your buds are matured, and you're ready to harvest. There are two ways to harvest your crop.

1 Partial harvest

Typically, buds nearer the light source will ripen before those lower down. So you can simply remove the top buds first, leaving the rest of the plant in situ to ripen over the coming days. This should not be an issue if you have cared for your plant during the flowering cycle and removed large leaves blocking light from reaching the buds.

HARVESTING TIP

If you opt for a full harvest, confine your scissors or knife to those main stems and side shoots that are heavy with bud. If you leave the rest of the plant intact, it may regenerate.

2 Full harvest

The alternative is to harvest the entire plant. Using a large pair of scissors, cut the plant near the base of the stem. Carefully remove it from the garden without disturbing any of the other plants.

HARVESTING AND CURING

Dirty work

Be warned that harvesting is smelly and dirty work, the more so the larger the crop you have. The smell of the resin given off as the buds are disturbed is enough to keep you floatin' for the remainder of the day. The sticky resin gets all over your fingers, permeates everything, and is very difficult to remove. Any clothes you wear for this process will be pretty much ready for the garbage afterward as will anything else the buds come into contact with. The golden rule is to cover or remove from the room anything you don't require, from furniture to pets. If kitty ends up with green fur and reeks of Cheech Marin's "aftershave," your girlfriend will never forgive you.

Slow death

From the moment you harvest your plants and they are separated from their root systems, they are dead. Hence their THC content can only decline from this point—it certainly does not increase, despite what you might have heard. Like a proud parent cosseting your offspring from the world, your goal from this point on is to protect your buds as much as possible and therefore slow the pace of THC degradation. This can be achieved by keeping the buds in undisturbed dark, dry, and warm conditions—less than 50 percent humidity and a maximum temperature of 80°F (26°C). (See "Care during drying" page 104.)

Manicuring

Now that you've plucked a beauty and have several branches full of ripe buds to gaze at, it's tempting just to roll a fat one right away. But these buds are a long way off from smoking. (They are too wet to smoke in this condition anyway.) First, they need manicuring.

Manicuring is a way of trimming the excess material from your buds, in preparation for drying. This can be done when the buds are wet (freshly cut) or dry. Manicuring when wet means that fewer of the THC-rich resin glands fall off; dry manicuring takes a lot less time though. Try manicuring over a silkscreen, if available, or at least always over glass or a table. That way you can gather up the stray resin glands that fall off during the process. Here's the manicuring process.

I Using a pair of scissors, cut the individual branches off the main stem.

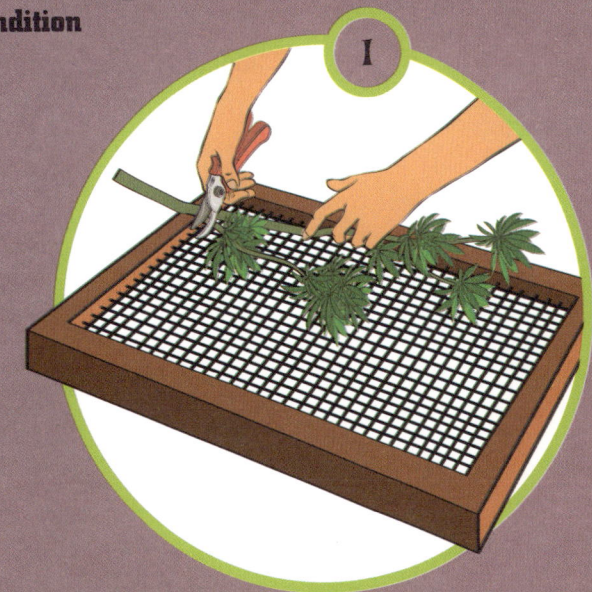

HARVESTING AND CURING

2 If necessary, depending on the size of your plant, trim these down further still. If you've managed to grow a behemoth outdoors, try to have no segment longer than 12 in. (30 cm) or 24 in. (60 cm). Then take each branch and trim the large fan leaves, followed by the smaller ones.

3 Soon you will be left with only juicy buds on the branch. Now that's a sight to behold.

Here you can clearly see the difference between a bud pre-manicure (left) and post-manicure (right). This process is fiddly, time-consuming, and messy but it is essential.

SEED TO WEED

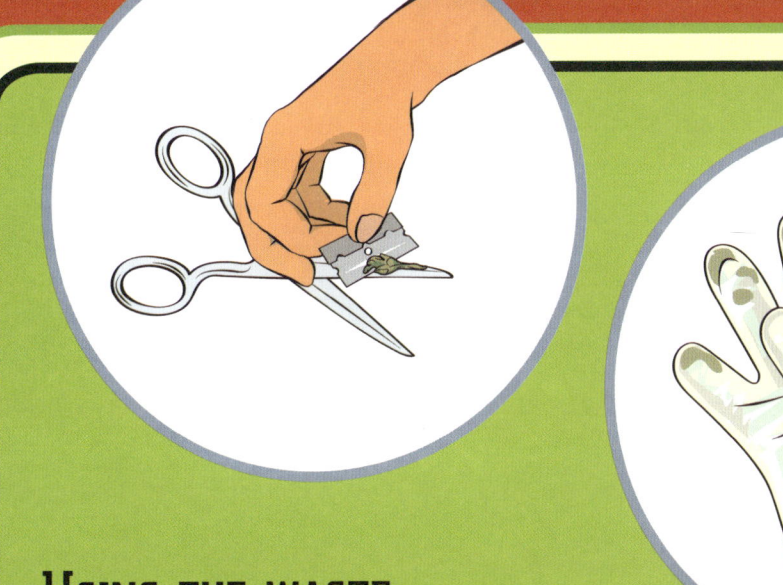

Using the waste

Don't just discard the spare leaves. Although the THC content is much lower than that in the buds, this can be made into hash at a later date. Similarly, take care to scrape away the resin that adheres to your scissors or knife. Wear cheap plastic gloves, such as those given away free with hair-dye kits. The gloves will be covered in resin by the end of the manicuring. Place them in the freezer overnight. In the morning scrape off the dried resin for smoking. These trichomes can be smoked later. Waste not want not!

SMOKE THE LEAF
Dried fan leaves make for a great substitute for tobacco in joints.

HARVESTING AND CURING

Drying

While it might smell sensational to trained nostrils and look highly inviting, the fresh, wet Mary Jane is not very potent and should never be smoked at this point. The science is too complex for your stoned mind to comprehend, so trust me when I say that a period of drying (the longer the better) at this stage helps to convert the THC into its proper mindblowing form.

Your babies should be dried slowly in controlled conditions to optimize the taste of your weed and the high it produces.

Do not eagerly pile your buds into the microwave and frazzle them or lay them outside in the sun on a hot day. Sure, this'll dry them, but not evenly; THC will not develop properly, and the smoke will taste harsh.

The drying room

A drying area can be built very simply. A closet, an unwanted small chest of drawers, or a wooden packing crate from a house move can be appropriated for this purpose. Or just build your own with a few pieces of MDF, a drill, and some screws. Let's assume you're using a packing crate. Read the instructions on the following pages to find out how to transform this humble object into your own drying "room."

1 First tidy the crate and wash it down. Lay it on its side on a table so you do not have to stoop to gain access.

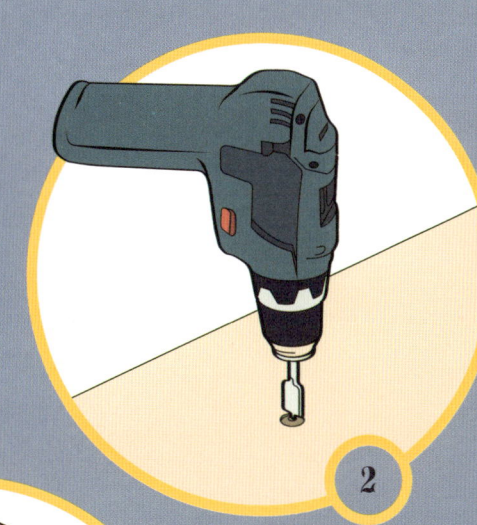

2 On opposite sides about 8 in. (20 cm) from the top and midway from each sides' edges, drill two holes large enough to run a length of wire (or string, cord, or washing line) through.

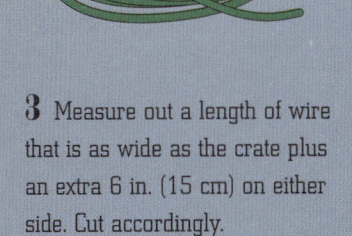

3 Measure out a length of wire that is as wide as the crate plus an extra 6 in. (15 cm) on either side. Cut accordingly.

HARVESTING AND CURING

103

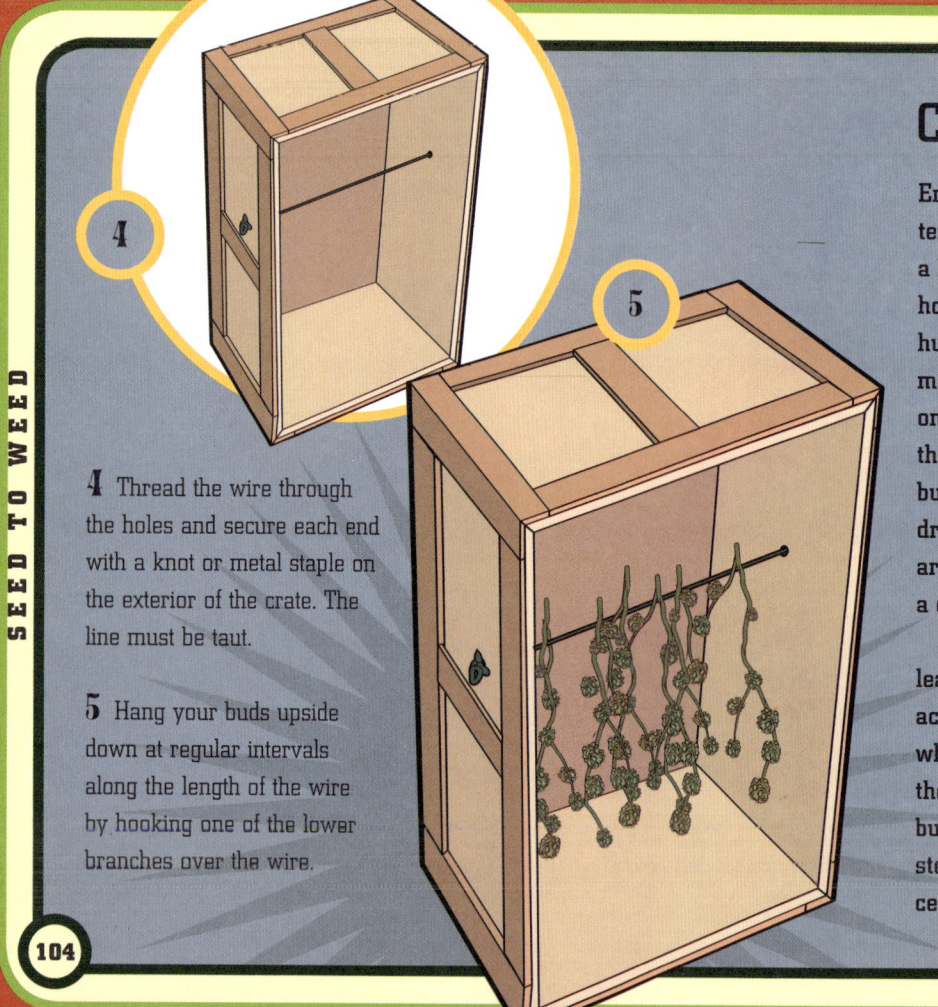

Care during drying

Ensure the room is kept at an even temperature of around 70°F (21°C) with a humidity of around 50 percent. Too hot and the buds will dry too fast; too humid and your crop may be subject to mold. Place a thermometer/hygrometer on the floor of the case to help monitor these levels. If you notice any signs of bud rot (see chapter 7) during the drying phase, then your conditions are too humid. Lower humidity with a circulation fan.

Leave your buds in this state for at least seven days. There are two fairly accurate checks you can make to gauge when your buds are ready. The buds themselves should feel dry to the touch but not brittle. And when you bend the stem, the outside will snap but the center stem will remain intact—if the

4 Thread the wire through the holes and secure each end with a knot or metal staple on the exterior of the crate. The line must be taut.

5 Hang your buds upside down at regular intervals along the length of the wire by hooking one of the lower branches over the wire.

The Stem Bending Test is a great way to gauge when your buds are through with the drying stage.

stem merely folds you should continue with the drying process; if it snaps completely it is over-dried.

Do not make these checks too regularly, however. Remember, every time you manhandle your stash, trichomes are lost and THC content reduces. Weed is for smoking, not playing with.

REHYDRATING

If you have made the mistake of over-drying your bud, fear not. Place the buds in a sealed jar overnight with a large fan leaf or some citrus peel inside. By the morning some of the moisture contained in the leaf or peel will have rehydrated your buds.

HARVESTING AND CURING

CURING

The curing stage is the final process your chronic goes through before it's ready to fire up. This might seem like an unnecessary delay, but there is a useful comparison here with another (legal) drug.

Some of the best wines in the world are drunk many years after they are bottled. So, too, fine cannabis matures with age. And while you don't have to wait years, another couple of weeks of curing will help the marijuana reach its peak.

Basically, curing sweats the bud, which allows it to retain its smell and flavor. And if you want the scientific explanation, it also aids the break down of chlorophyll, which, being magnesium-rich, causes that raspy taste in the back of your throat that's associated with smoking fresh bud.

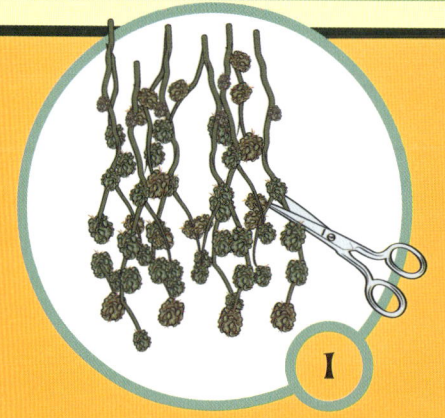

Great growers have established that a period of two months of combined drying and curing produces marijuana at peak performance. Buds cured for longer than this will lose potency as cannabinoids change composition after this time.

Follow these three steps to cure the buds:

1 When your buds are dry, take them down from the hanging wire and, using a pair of scissors, gently cut them from the stems and branches. This waste can be discarded or used for hash making.

2 Place the buds carefully in an airtight glass or metal container. Leave a generous amount of space at the top of the container so the buds can breathe.

Storing

If you're not ready to smoke your weed yet, you should store it in the refrigerator or freezer where it will be perfectly okay for several months, even years. Under no condition should you store your bud in the soft plastic bags that dealers frequently use. Because of electric attraction, resin glands are drawn to the plastic, never to be recovered, so a lot of the THC will be lost. You'll be left wondering why your buddy, who kept his stash in a glass jar, is getting a lot higher than you.

However, given that you've been itching to smoke this chronic since you first spied a bud a couple of days into flowering, storing is probably not in your thoughts. Now is finally the time you can send your first crop up in smoke. Roll a fat one, spark it up, inhale deeply, and reflect on a job well done.

But idle hands make for the devil's work, didn't ya know? There's more growing to be done if you want more where this came from.

3 Place the container in a cool, dry, dark place. Every day, remove the lid for a couple of hours to allow moisture to escape. Every couple of days, move the buds around in the jar.

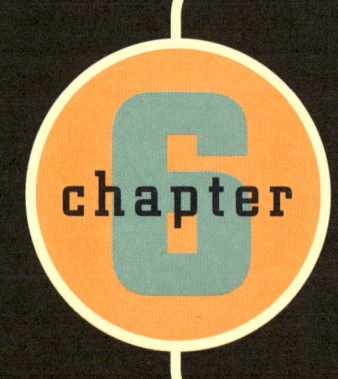

chapter 6
STARTING OVER

"Dope will get you through times of no money better than money will get you through times of no dope."

—Fabulous Furry Freak Brothers

If you're anything like me, the first thought that'll cross your mind as you're curing your buds is where the next batch is coming from. Once you've been bitten by the growing bug, you'll want to try again. There are two ways for the burgeoning gardener to grow pot the second time around. Both involve growing more plants, but in different ways.

New Seeds

Of course, you *can* just buy more seeds. But as previously explained, these are expensive. It's also lazy. If your previous grow was successful, you liked the buzz it gave, and you want to repeat it, your best bet is to acquire seeds from existing plants. You must be patient with this method, however, because the plant will need to go through its entire life cycle before you can get the seeds.

You will need to establish a separate growing environment that contains both males and females. Essentially you follow the same process as with sinsemilla, but this time, you allow the males to fertilize the females during the flowering stage. When the female eventually dies, the seeds will fall to the floor.

This may seem like a lot of time with no bud at the end of it, but you could have hundreds of seeds from one plant! These can be stored for at least a couple of years in an airtight camera film canister or vitamin container, placed in the freezer. Be sure to label it with a name and date—you know how bad your memory is.

Mother Plant

The alternative method to growing from seed is to use clones. This entails growing a mother plant. If you are growing from feminized seeds, you can be pretty sure you are growing a female from the outset. If you are growing from regular seeds, weed out the males as soon as they show their sex at preflowering, just as you would do with sinsemilla.

The major difference from this point on is that you maintain the 18/6 or 24/0 photoperiod. In this way, you do not allow the mother plant to enter the flowering stage but keep it instead in a permanent vegetative state. This mother plant should be kept in a separate location. To grow more sinsemilla, just take a cutting (or clone) of the mother plant as described in "Cloning," page 112.

Nutrient tip: Give your mother plant about 10 percent less nitrogen than your other flowering plants as this promotes root growth in clones.

Taking clones from a mother plant is quicker than growing from seed. Clones can be harvested in about three months, whereas seeds will take four to five months to mature. Plus, of course, with clones you can have guaranteed sinsemilla. With regular seeds, half your crop will prove to be irksome males.

Dos and don'ts

Do not take clones from mother plants that are less than two months old. Cloning prior to this will lead to weak clones. Clones don't have to be taken from females in a vegetative state. You can take cuttings from flowering females. On the plus side, clones root quickly, but the down side is that they will take a month or so to revert back to the vegetative stage and this undue stress can lead to disease.

STARTING OVER

Cloning

You will need some further equipment to make clones, in addition to the standard grow-room setup (see box for a list of these items). Prepare all of this before you start and clear a large area in which to work. Tidy up! Pretend your mother-in-law is visiting. For instance, if you make a cutting only to find your rooting medium is buried beneath a stack of DVDs, it'll be dead before you know it.

Step-by-step cloning

Follow this 13-point plan to clone effectively.

1 Identify a clone toward the bottom of the mother plant where the branches are more rigid. The clone should be 2–4 in. (5–10 cm) tall with plenty of leaves.

Here's the material you'll need:

- Rooting medium (e.g., rock wool, Oasis root cubes, Jiffy)
- Rooting hormone (liquid or gel)
- Disinfectant (alcohol or bleach)
- Glass of water
- Razor or sharp scissors
- Humidity dome
- Small pot
- pH tester
- Heating mat

3 Place the cutting on a flat, clean surface. Trim off any lower leaves where the node meets the stem. Clones that have several exposed nodes below the rooting medium tend to flourish better.

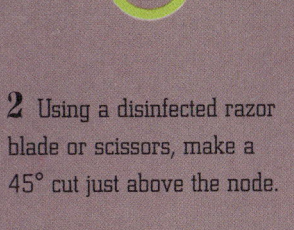

2 Using a disinfected razor blade or scissors, make a 45° cut just above the node.

4 Cut the remaining leaves in half. This will allow less surface area for the plants to breathe and prevent them from overlapping.

STARTING OVER

6 Place your rooting medium in the pot. Using a sterilized pencil or nail, make a hole in the center of the medium that is slightly larger than the clone's stem.

5 Cut the stem at a 45° angle just below a node—this will expose the maximum area for rooting. Immediately transfer the cutting to a glass of pH balanced water (pH 5–6) to prevent it from wilting.

7 Cover the stem of your clone in rooting liquid/gel. (Follow the product's instructions for greater guidance.)

8 Gently lower the stem into the hole, leaving a gap of about ½ in. (1 cm) at the bottom of the rooting medium to allow for root growth, and carefully pack the rooting medium around it to hold in place.

SIGNS OF TROUBLE

A little wilting of your clones in the first couple of days is normal; after all, the cuttings were happily attached to the mother plant until very recently, and you have badly stressed them out. Within three or four days they should have forgiven you and will look a good deal perkier, but clones that continue to wilt after seven days or show little sign of rooting are probably done for. You should discard these and start again. However, yellowing leaves are not necessarily bad news. Plants instinctively direct all their resources to growing new roots at the expense of some lower leaves. So, as long as root growth looks okay, a few dying leaves is not a problem.

STARTING OVER

9 Water the clone lightly but regularly, especially for the first few days. The medium needs to be kept evenly moist but not soggy.

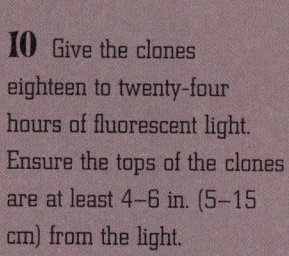

10 Give the clones eighteen to twenty-four hours of fluorescent light. Ensure the tops of the clones are at least 4–6 in. (5–15 cm) from the light.

11 Clones need close to 100 percent humidity for the first couple of days after cutting. Reduce to 80 percent after three to four days. A propagator (or humidity tent) is a good option, and this can either be bought or fashioned from rigid plastic or glass. Ensure there are vent holes so that your cuttings can breathe. Mist your clones several times a day. This enables them to retain moisture in the absence of any roots.

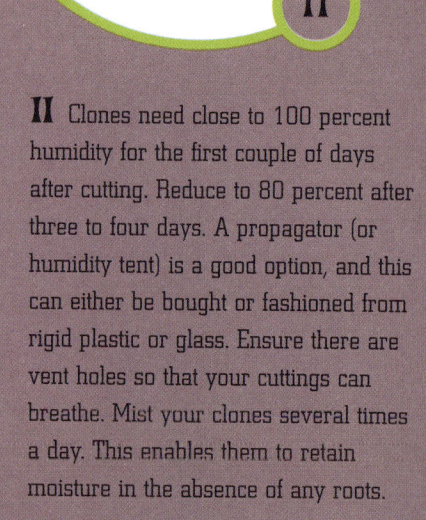

12 Root growth is heightened if the rooting medium is warmer than the air temperature. Use a heating mat to keep the growing medium at around 75°F–80°F (24°C–26.5°C).

13 After seven days, the clone should be showing signs of root growth, but do not disturb the clone unduly to check for this. After twenty days, roots should be clearly visible through the bottom and sides of the pot and the clone is ready for transplanting and transferring to the vegetative photoperiod. Then follow the steps described in chapters 4 and 5.

STARTING OVER

Regeneration

If you don't wish to grow from seeds (no patience, eh?) or are too lazy to invest in a mother plant, there is a third option open to indoor growers—regeneration (basically reusing your flowered plant). To regenerate a cannabis plant, you must not brutalize the plant when harvesting of course. Remove only the upper buds and allow the stems, fan leaves, and lower buds to remain.

Reset your lighting setup to the 24/0 vegetative stage and feed the plant with nitrogen-rich food. For hydroponic grows, drain the "bloom" nutrient solution from the tank and replace it with the vegetative mix.

Within a week or two you should notice some new growth. All being well, maintain the vegetative state until you're ready to flower. Providing your plant is well cared for, this process can be repeated several times to good effect.

A Professional Setup

Remember your simple indoor grow box from chapter 3? Well here's a more sophisticated example (if you can call the introduction of a shelf "sophisticated") that will serve you well in your continuing growing career. You've come a long way since your days as a virgin of cannabis cultivation, and if your first grow was even moderately successful, this is the next natural step.

The beauty of this setup is that you can have a continual harvest every sixty to seventy days. The bottom tier is set to vegetative growth (18/6 or 24/0) while the upper tier is set to flowering mode (12/12). You have to ensure that the light from the lower area does not leak into the higher flowering area, so the dividing shelf must be fully lightproofed.

If you are well organized, you should be in a position to flower your seedlings as soon as the plants on the upper tier are harvested. Who'd have thought it could be so easy. . . .

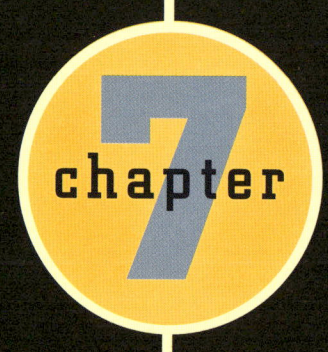

chapter 7
TROUBLESHOOTING

"Two of my favorite things are sitting on my front porch smoking a pipe of sweet hemp, and playing my Hohner harmonica."

Abraham Lincoln

Despite weed being considered pretty easy to grow, it's not all smooth sailing. Cannabis does react badly to poor conditions and is prone to diseases and bug infestations. As a first-time grower, it's likely you will unwittingly cause your plants some stress. As counseling is not an option for them, pay attention here to avoid making their lives a misery.

Environmental Problems

The most frequent cause of distress for marijuana plants is an issue with their environment. For all their supposed hardiness, marijuana plants, particularly those cultivated indoors, can be fickle things. They're either too hot or too cold, too damp or too dry, suffering from an excess or deficiency of nutrients, or their pH level is off. And as you are their sole carer I'm sorry to say their distress is something you will have caused. Talk about hurting the ones you love. But before you get too teary-eyed, follow this chart to diagnose your plants' condition and find out how to make them better.

Symptom	Cause
Slow growth and curled-down leaves	Lack of ventilation
Spindly growth; stretching between internodes	Lack of light or light too far from the plants
Burned patches on leaves	Lights too close to plants
Slow growth and drooping leaves	Temperature too high
Slow growth, refusal to flower	Temperature too low
Nutrient deficiencies, wilting	Under- or overwatering/feeding

Healthy leaf

pH Problems

Just as a human being who lives off junk food and eats few if any fruits and vegetables (sound familiar?) will probably suffer from health problems, so marijuana plants that don't get the correct nutrients will get "ill."

If your pH is straying from neutral and your plants look in less than tiptop shape, then you probably have nutrient issues.

Check out the table opposite and the accompanying illustrations to help you figure out their malady.

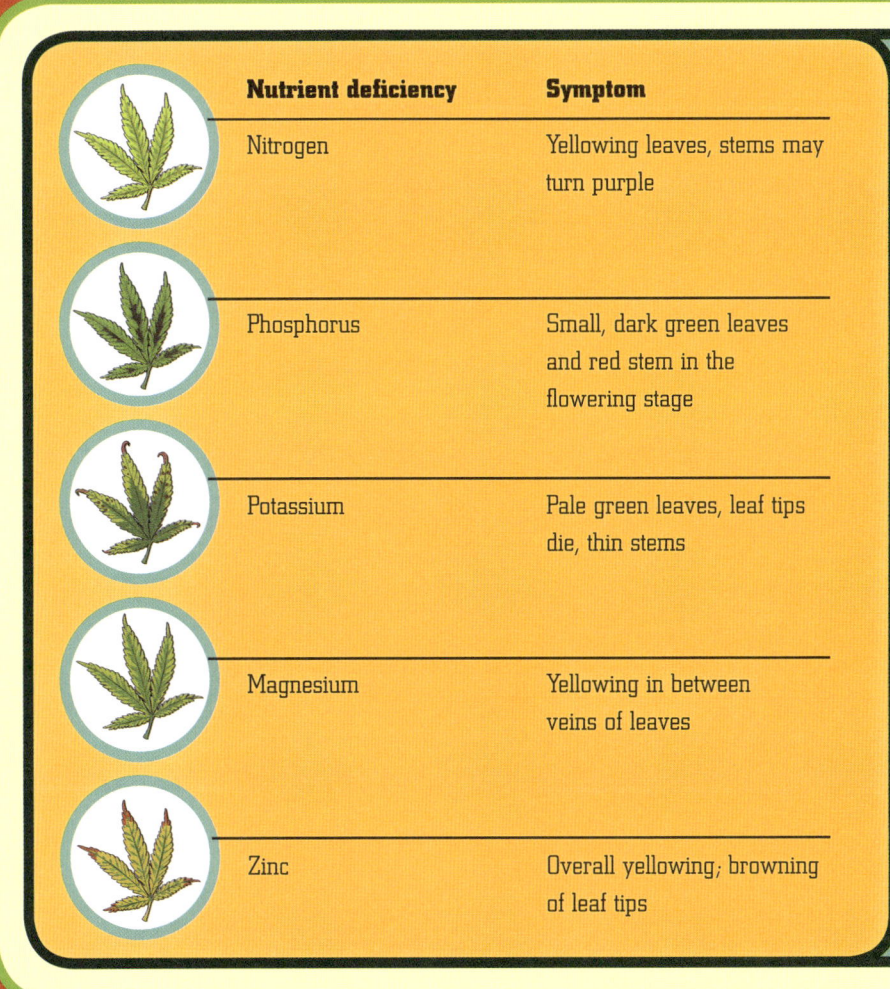

Nutrient deficiency	Symptom
Nitrogen	Yellowing leaves, stems may turn purple
Phosphorus	Small, dark green leaves and red stem in the flowering stage
Potassium	Pale green leaves, leaf tips die, thin stems
Magnesium	Yellowing in between veins of leaves
Zinc	Overall yellowing; browning of leaf tips

Leaching

Nutrient deficiencies are not your only problem; your plants can also become overfertilized. Adding calcium to the growing medium will help to balance the pH. If the situation requires more drastic action, you can *leach* (or flush) your pots. Place the plants in a bathtub or sink and soak them through with a generous amount of tap water (about three times the amount of water to soil). Allow the water to drain through, and dry the pots out over the coming days. The impurities in the soil should have been washed through.

TROUBLESHOOTING

Get Clean

Not clean from drugs obviously, that would be a terrible waste of a good crop, but, do introduce cleanliness to your garden (and yourself) to give your plants the best chance of remaining healthy. The worst thing to beset any garden is an infestation. Insects are present outdoors of course, but while they are kept in check in that environment, they can have a field day in the hostile-free indoor garden. So, follow some basic rules:

- Never waltz straight from mowing the grass in your backyard to check in on your grow room—you're asking for trouble.
- Keep all tools and surfaces clean.
- Wash your hands and wear clean clothes.
- Keep pets and other houseplants at bay.
- Don't visit the garden unnecessarily.
- Washing your grow area with a 5 percent bleach solution between grows is also highly recommended.

You can probably stop short of wearing a hygiene facemask, unless paying due respect to the late great King of Pop, but you get the point. The fewer outside agencies that come into contact with your garden the better . . . especially the FBI.

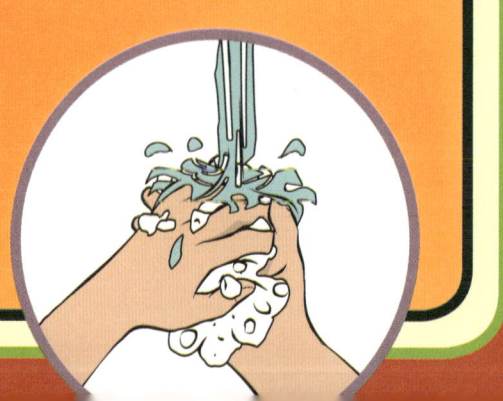

Pesticide Safety!

Only use pesticides that are clearly marked for "Food Product Use." Otherwise you will end up poisoning your bud. If it's not safe for food, and therefore not intended to be ingested, it's certainly not meant to be inhaled! **Take extreme care**.

Hit 'Em Early

Any bugs that are detected are best tackled in the vegetative stage when the plant is more durable. Use caution when treating flowering plants as the buds can react badly.

PESTS AND FUNGUS

Sometimes the inevitable will happen, and your plants will get sick. Many of the symptoms of a pest attack are similar to those associated with under- or over-watering, nutrient deficiencies, or temperature issues. The best way to determine if you have pests is to see the little blighters. So a magnifying glass is once again a useful tool. Here's a list of some leading Enemies of the Pot Grower and advice on how to hit 'em where it hurts.

Aphids

This is the most common pest faced by growers and your "Most Wanted." An aphid is the bin Laden of the insect world. Aphids live off plant juices by sucking the sap. (Do not try this yourself; it will not get you high, trust me.) They're about 1/8 in. (3 mm) long and commonly yellow-green although the darned chameleons can be any color. The foamy waste they secrete is called honeydew, which sounds delicious but almost certainly isn't.

Kill 'em by washing leaves with a soapy pesticide and/or introducing ladybugs (a natural predator of aphids) to the garden.

Spider mites

Spider mites are real tiny critters who gather in clusters and spin webs, hence their name, and, like aphids, they live off the plant's juice.

Kill 'em by using specialist pesticides, soaps, or sulphur.

TROUBLESHOOTING

125

Whiteflies

These are small flies that are white—no shit. There are more than two hundred varieties of this species, but we don't expect you to know all of them! If you shake your plant, you'll hear them before you see them, and they can trash a crop quicker than Axl Rose can waste a hotel room. Their honeydew can develop into dark mold.

Kill 'em by introducing spiders, ladybugs, and beetles and/or using sticky pest tape, general sprays, and soaps.

Thrips

Thrips have minute, dark-colored bodies, and the adults can fly. They usually attack the buds, causing them to fall apart and look silvery.

Kill 'em by using natural predators like beetles and ladybugs and/or thrip pesticide. Like vampires, they also don't like garlic spray (cans of this are available in stores). So make pretend you're Buffy when you slay these critters.

Bud rot

Fungus botrytis, to give it its proper name, is the most common variety of fungus. It starts as a white, powdery growth and turns gray as it spreads. It affects the leaves and the flowers. If ignored or undetected, it can wipe out a crop in a few days. In severe cases culling these stricken plants may be the only way to save some of the harvest.

Kill it by using fungicide, lowering humidity levels and increasing ventilation to stop it spreading, and cutting away affected areas.

Mildew

Powdery mildew

Similar to bud rot, this fungus is easier to wipe off than *botrytis* but spreads more quickly, covering the plants in a white film. This mildew inhibits photosynthesis and stunts the plant's growth.

Kill it by following the notes opposite in "Bud rot."

OUTDOOR PESTS

Outdoor pests tend to be of the larger variety and can include deer, rabbits, and rodents. Keep these animals at bay with secure fencing, and ring your crop with urine—but not in front of people, you filthy devil! If you're suffering from any of these pests in your indoor garden, then you have far greater issues in your life than whether your cannabis garden reaps a good harvest. And don't use the urine indoors; it'll make a bad situation worse.

Pet trouble

Keep pets, especially cats, away from your garden. Kittens will be tempted to play with the leaves, and cats of all ages will use the base as a litter tray. That's the sort of fertilizer your plants don't need!

WHAT'S WRONG?

With all these potential causes of distress for your plant, how do you tell the cause? The honest answer is experience, but if your plant is affected in sporadic areas while other portions are fine, this is likely to be an insect attack. Nutrient deficiencies will attack the plant in a linear form from the bottom up. There may be nothing you can do. There are a lot of bad seeds on the market, and if you have bought a strain with dodgy genetics, the only solution is to acquire better seeds next time.

TROUBLESHOOTING

ACKNOWLEDGMENTS

The author would like to thank: Will Steeds and Laura Ward at Elephant Book Company; Lindsey Johns for the great look of the pages; Jeff Ditchfield for help with the text; and Rob Brandt for making sense of the reference once again to produce some super illustrations.